London International Conferences

PROCEEDINGS 2021-4

September 2021

4th London International Conference, 04 September 2021, hosted online by UKEY Consulting and Publishing, London, United Kingdom

LONDONIC.UK

ISBN: 9798480457506

Proceedings: 4th London International Conference, September 2021

Authors:
Akif Celepcikay
Albert Efendi Pohan
Alwan Hadiyanto
Bambang Sugiyono Agus Purwono
Begench Soyunov
Christina Schabasser
Dhenny Asmarazisa Azis
Elsa Putri Ermisah Syafril
Emin Alp Arslan
Ibrahim Bisen
İbrahim Kurt
Kamil Yildirim
M. Fahim Tharaba
Mehmet Ali Eroğlu
Rosida Kerin Meirani
Shyamala Susan
Taushanzhi Constantine
Yetkin Yildirim

Design:	**Studio Ima**
Cover:	**ITACon**
Publisher:	**UKEY Publishing**
Version:	**V01**
Series:	**Proceedings 04**

Copyright © 2021 UKEY publishing
ukeyconsultingpublishing.co.uk

ISBN: 9798480457506

Content

London International Conferences

londonic.uk   ukeyconsultingpublishing.co.uk

Evolution Human Resources Management Ulu Al-Albab in The New Era

M Fahim Tharaba
Universitas Islam Negeri Maulana Malik Ibrahim, Malang,
Indonesia
fahimuinmaliki@gmail.com

Bambang Sugiyono Agus Purwono
State Polytechnic of Malang, Indonesia

Shyamala Susan
APC Mahalaxmi College for Women, Thoothukudi, Tamilnadu,
India

Rosida Kerin Meirani
Universitas Islam Negeri Maulana Malik Ibrahim, Malang,
Indonesia

Abstract

In this era of industry 4.0 or disruption which becomes global, where the effect of technology especially information, communication, and transportation runs rapidly, it is very difficult to find Ulu al-albab profile that really can be standard in the al-Qur'an because Ulu al-albab is not only intellectual, but also emotional spiritual ability. The focus of this research is to find out the evolution human resources management ulu

al-albab in the new era is developed at the State Islamic
University of Maulana Malik Ibrahim (UIN Malang) Malang,
Indonesia. This research method is qualitative approach. The
results of the research are: The philosophy of ulu al-albab
perspective developed by the UIN Malang is actually the same
as the term of spirituality, with the ulul albab method that
produces: (a) Morals, (b) Spiritual, (c) Science, and (d)
Professionalism; which is associated with mind, heart,
intellect, insight, understanding, wisdom, with strategy,
namely: (a) Increasing integration; (b) Sharpening sensitivity;
(c) Ensuring relevance; (d) Developing; and (e) Maintaining
independence.

Keywords: evolution, human resources management,
philosophy of ulu al-albab, spirituality

Fahim Tharaba
B. S. A. Purwono
Shyamala Susan
R. Kerin Meirani

Introduction

In this era of industry 4.0 or disruption which becomes global, where the effect of technology especially information and communication and transportation runs rapidly, it is very difficult to find Ulu al-albab profile that really can be standard in the al-Qur'an because Ulu al-albabis not only intellectual, but also emotional spiritual ability [1]. The philosophy of ulu al-albab perspective developed by the UIN Malang is actually the same as the term of spirituality, with the ulul albab method that produces: (a) Morals, (b) Spiritual, (c) Science, and (d) Professionalism.

Research Method

This research needs the deep observation in the natural setting which is known as qualitative approach [2,3] as stated as: "…..naturalistic approach in education field." The steps of this research are firstly, data collection of the site of the research (UIN Malang) as the subject. The data entered are observed, coded and made by seeing the categories developed in a theme. Secondly, based on the conceptual result of the subject, it made the analysis by making conceptual development which was resulted by the subject. By these steps, the steady conceptual result can be obtained and can be abstracted deeply about the Evolution Human Resources Management ulu al-albab in the New Era in the site of the research. To reveal the last result, modified analytic induction is applied as the way to develop and verify the theory.

Evolution And Revolution Human Resourches Management Ulu Al-Albab In Reality

Since 2011, Industry Revolution 4.0 had socialized in the world, and next step is Society 5.0, including in education sector. Teaching and learning also changed according to future orientation. Changing in literacy revolution (e.g.: *reading, writing, & aritmathic* shifted to the data literation, technology, human). Society 5.0 drives the Information revolution, digitalization in all human sectors. Emerge he Covid 19 Pandemic and New Normal [4].

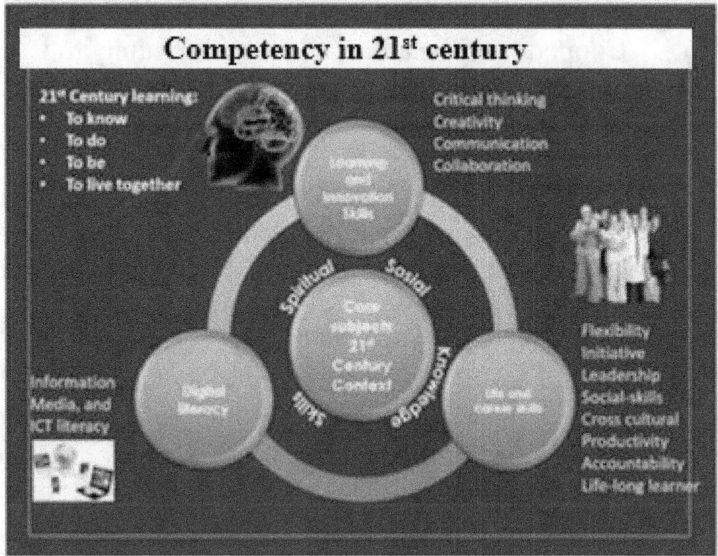

Figure 1. Revolution and Evolution Human Resources Management between Covid 19 Pandemic & New Normal [4]

The Education challenges in e future:

1. In the future will be set up the foreign high education will be launched in Indonesia (e.g Harvard University, Sidney University, California University).
2. Emerge the disruptive innovation in education by online and distance learning massive (impact of Covid 19 Pandemic).
3. Increasing Teaching and Learning Process using the digital technology (Online system)
4. Increasing the quality cost of lecturers recruitment and reward.

5. Increasing the commitment of the humanity and national value in every teaching and learning process.

While the school plays the role of applying character education within (1) combining teachers, parents and students altogether to emphasize the character they want; (2) Train teachers to integrate character education into the life and school culture, (3) Cooperate with parents and the community to teach students on how character behavior is important for success in school and in life, and (4) The principal, teachers, parents and community should get the opportunity to be a model of social and moral attitudes. Contrary to the concept of holistic approach and continued with the efforts made by the school, it can be understood that the process of character education must be carried out continuously (continually) so that the moral values that have been embedded in the child's personal not only to a certain level of education or only appear in the family or community environment only. In addition, the moral practices of children do not seem to be formality, but are completely embedded in the child's soul.

To realize the ongoing character education (continually) is to require models of integrated character education, namely: integration into the learning process in all subjects, student coaching activities, and the culture and management of schools.

1. Spiritual and emotional development,

2. Intellectual development,

3. Physical and kinesthetic development, and

4. Affective and creativity development [5]

Thomas Lickona (1992) said three elements of good character, namely:

1. Noble knowing or knowledge of morals,

2. Noble feeling or feelings about morals and

3. Noble action or moral acts.

Fahim Tharaba
B. S. A. Purwono
Shyamala Susan
R. Kerin Meirani

Students are able to understand, feel and work on the values of virtue:

1.Spiritual depth,

2.Moral nobility,

3.The breadth of science,

4.Professional maturity [5]

Ali Imron [4] stated that: "Key Success Factors in the 4th Industrial Revolution Era (see Figure 2)."

Also, Ali Imron [4] stated that: "Cultivate human-tech literacy resources in the 4th IR Era (see Figure 3)."

Finally, development strategy Model of Ulū al-Albāb-based science integration will be integrated with institutional while traversed with the development of the tree of sciences with four processes, namely: (a) deepening of spirituality, (b) the determination/improvement of morality, (c) Expansion/mastery of intellectuality, and (d) the maturation of professionalism.[6]

Fahim Tharaba
B. S. A. Purwono
Shyamala Susan
R. Kerin Meirani

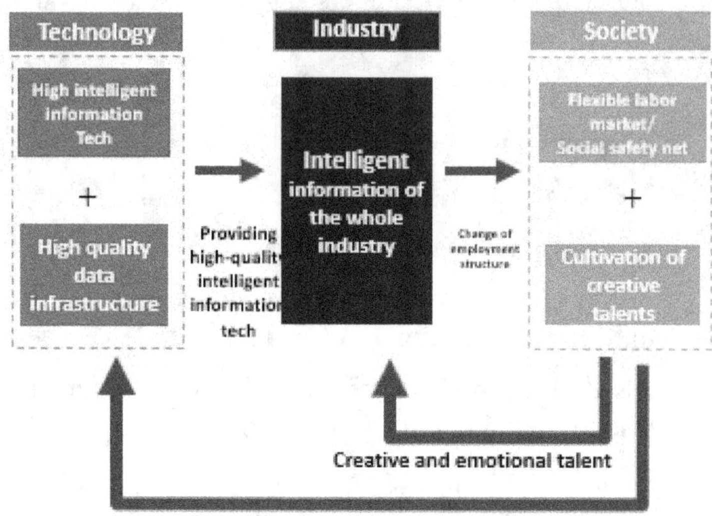

Figure 2. Key Success Factors in the 4th Industrial Revolution Era

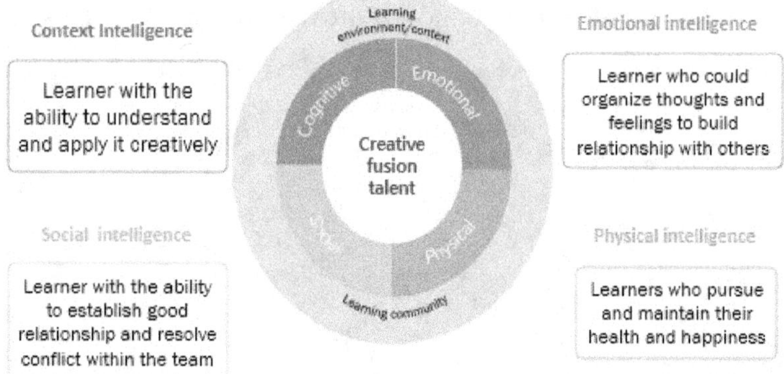

Figure 3. Cultivate human-tech literacy resources in the 4th IR Era

Fahim Tharaba
B. S. A. Purwono
Shyamala Susan
R. Kerin Meirani

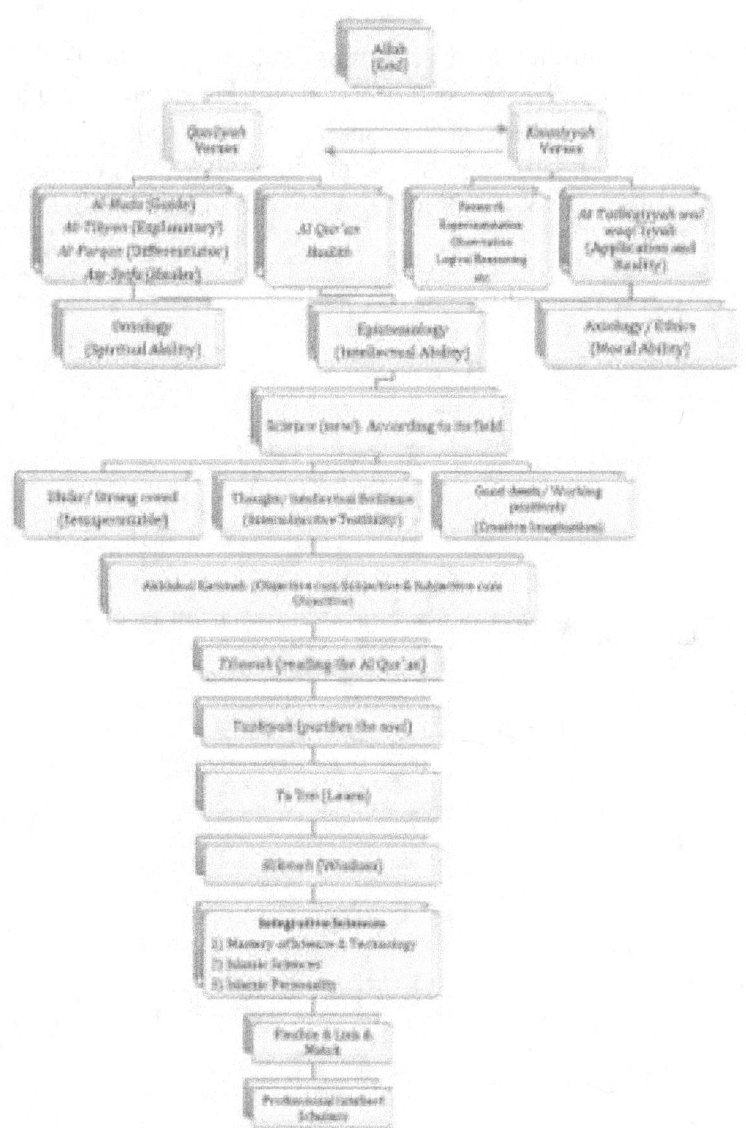

Figure 4. Science Integration Development strategy flow chart

Conclusion:

Evolution human resources management ulu al-albab in the new era can be standard in the al-Qur'an because Ulu al-alba is not only intellectual, but also emotional spiritual ability, with the ulul albab method that produces: 1. Spiritual depth, 2. Moral nobility, 3.The breadth of science, 4. Professional maturity.

References:

[1] Tharaba, MF, Zulfi Mubarog, Ali Nasith, BSA Purwono. 2021. The Science Integrational Ulu al-abab Perspective (Campus Development toward World Class University. Journal of Psychology and Education. Vol 58, no. 1, pp. 1284-1291. *ISSN: 00333077.*

[2] R.C, Bogdan,and S.K. Biklen, 1982.*Qualitative Research Education: an Introduction to Theory and Methode*, London, Allin & Bacon, Inc.

[3] Denzin, NK, and Lincoln, YS, 1994. *Handbook of Qualitative Research.* Thousand Oaks, Clifornia: SAGE Publications, Inc.

[4] Imron Arifin, Pengembangan Manajemen Pendidikan Islam Di Era Revolusi Industri 4.0 Dan New Normal, Webinar Pengembangan MPI di Era Industri 4.0, Konsorsium Manajemen Pendidikan Islam (MPI), UIN Maulana Malik Ibrahim Malang, Gedung Rektorat Lt.4 Ruang LPM UIN Maliki Malang, Senin, 01 Maret 2021/ 03 Jumadil Tsaniyah 1442 H.

[5] M. Fahim Tharaba, et. all. Character Building Through Language Learning And Culture Of Islamic Boarding School In Terms Of The Implementation Of Management Towards Sustainable Development Of Green Campus, **Jilin Daxue Xuebao (Gongxueban)/Journal of Jilin University (Engineering and Technology Edition)** ISSN : 1671-5497 E-Publication Online Open Access Vol: 40 Issue: 05-2021 DOI:10.17605/OSF.IO/ZFKDY.

[6] M. Fahim Tharaba, et. all. The Development Of Science Integration Towards Smart Campuses In Indonesia Using The Islamic Higher Education Management Model, Tianjin Daxue Xuebao (Ziran Kexue yu Gongcheng Jishu Ban)/Journal of Tianjin University Science and Technology, ISSN (Online): 0493-2137, E-Publication: Online Open Access, Vol:54 Issue:06:2021. DOI:10.17605/OSF.IO/QBZV3

London International Conferences

londonic.uk

CONSULTING & PUBLISHING

ukeyconsultingpublishing.co.uk

Analysis of the Influence of Business Opportunities, Shopping, Transportation, Safety, Clean Environment, and Government Services on City Brand Attitude and Intention to Continue Living Satellite City Population

Begench Soyunov
Faculty of Economics and Business
Airlangga University

Abstract

Satellite cities are supporting cities of the major city, such as Gresik, Sidoarjo and Surabaya. The goal of this research is to look for factors that affect city brand attitude toward satellite City Brand image and need to find whether there is positive effect between City Brand attitude to the intention to continue living in the cities especially for those who live in Gresik City and Sidoarjo City. Sample of this research was incomer residents who live in Gresik and Sidoarjo and work in Surabaya.

Data were gathered and analyzed using Structural Equation Modelling – AMOS. The findings of this research shows that there was a positive and significant effect between business opportunity and clean environment to the city brand attitude in satellite cities. Moreover, both Gresik and Sidoarjo City has a same result that there was a positive and significant effect between city brand attitude and intention to continue living in the city. The discussion begins with descriptive statistical results that aims to understand the profile of the respondents used in this study. Followed by a discussion of the research instruments testing that includes testing the validity and reliabilities. This is done to ensure the research data obtained, so that quality can be significantly justified.

Then followed by analysis goodness of fit criteria and their research model is a discussion of the results testing Structural Equation Modelling (SEM), which aims to clarify the relationship between the hypothesized variables. Profile of respondents aim to know the characteristics of respondents. Respondents in this study were residents of suburbs around the city of Surabaya. Respondents from the study will be profile based on gender, age, education, past employment, and monthly expenditure. In the discussion of the research results, will explain the test results the hypothesized relationship between the variables. Thus, there are ten (10) a discussion that will be explained. Here's an explanation for each of the hypothesized relationship between the variables.

Keywords: Satellite Cities, City Brand attitude, City Brand attributee, Intention to living

London International Conferences

londonic.uk

ukeyconsultingpublishing.co.uk

Virtualization of Teacher Training on Improving of Online Teaching Competence for the Students of Riau Island University in Indonesia

Albert Efendi Pohan
Yogyakarta State University, Yogyakarta, Indonesia
albertefendi.2020@student.uny.ac.id

Alwan Hadiyanto
Riau Island University, Batam City, Indonesia
alwan.hadiyanto@gmail.com

Dhenny Asmarazisa Azis
Riau Island University, Batam City, Indonesia
dhennyasmarazisa@gmail.com

Abstract

The purpose of this study is to measure the effect of the virtual training to improve the students online teaching competence. The subjects of this study were students of the faculty of teaching and education about 16 students. To achieve the objectives of this research, mix method with the exploratory sequential was adopted. This research consists of qualitative and quantitative with the pre-experimental design. The qualitative data were analyzed by data collection, data reduction, data display and conclusion. While the quantitative data were analyzed by using the application of Statistical

Product and Service Solution (SPSS) version 21. The qualitative finding showed that the students online teaching competence was very low both of competence in designing lesson plan and online teaching practice before they followed the virtual training. The quantitative finding showed that the virtual training has the significant effect to improve the students where the significant designing lesson plan value (2-tailed) is 0.00 < 0.5 and online teaching competence value (2-tailde) is 0.00 < 0.05. Thus, virtual training can improve the students online teaching competence in the English education study program at the University of Riau Island Indonesia.

Keywords: Competence, Improve, Online Learning, Virtual Training

1. Introduction

Teacher competence is the ability of teachers to perform their self to do the main tasks in a procedural ways to achieve educational goals institutionally and nationally. Based on the law number 20 of 2003 mentioned that the main tasks of the teachers in Indonesia consist of 3 part, designing the learning preparations, teaching practice by applying the relevant strategy and method, and evaluating learning process. To achieve results of the learning process based on the goals stated before effectively, teachers are required have the high competence and professional in doing their tasks regularly. According to Siri et al (2020) competent teachers are they have strong knowledge about the field of study being taught, has the right attitude about oneself, school, peers, and the field of study fostered, has good skills in teaching techniques actually in implementing strategy and learning method, and mastering the education technology used. This is in line with Abusomwan and Osaigbovo (2020) define that the teacher competencies include the ability to use learning methods and strategies, effective classroom management, motivating skills, evaluation strategies, preparation of learning plans and the effective use of teaching materials. In this case the teachers' ability to organize online and non-online learning need to be comprehend.

Improving teacher competence must be a serious priority in conducting online learning at this time due to the impact of the Covid-19 pandemic which has stopped the face-to-face learning process from being online (Nic Beech, 2020). Plans, systems and learning processes undergo a total change (Jacob et al, 2021) and these changes have an impact on policy making, parents, students and educational institutions. The changing of the learning system occur in the learning process from traditional classroom-based teaching to the virtual learning approaches (Mseleku, 2020). This condition has caused some serious problem where the learning process could not run effectively in all countries, especially in Indonesia. The research of Tarkar's (2020) showed that parents are not proficient in using online learning technology to accompany their children to take part in online learning. Furthermore, Napitupulu (2020) revealed that 63% of students in Indonesia could not participate in online learning because of the low ability of teachers to master online learning technology so that the learning process was dominant by giving assignments to students. This information was in line with the research results of Mursalin, et al (2021) that 42.22% of teachers were not ready for online learning because teachers have low competence (Egert, Dederer, & Fukkink, 2020).

The problems mentioned above indicated that all components of education need to participate to offer the effective and efficient solutions. In this case, universities in the field of education should be contribute to preparing student as the teacher candidates who have competencies which relevant to the needs of the current learning system today. By understanding the urgency of the problems stated above, the researcher contributed through this research with the title Virtualization of Teacher Training on Improving of Online Teaching Competence for the Students of Riau Island University In Indonesia. This training aimed to improve the students' competence in online teaching needs to be carried out to equip students with the skills to use technology in online learning.

1.2. Literature Review

Teachers' Competence

Based on the Law of the Republic of Indonesia Number 14 of 2005 concerning Teachers and Lecturers, competence is a set of knowledge, skills, and behaviors that must be possessed, internalized, and controlled by a teacher or lecturer who carries out his professional duties. Competence is a person's ability to carry out their main tasks effectively in accordance with his field (Qomariah, 2020). This is in line with Sunyoto (2015) defines competence is the skill to do their duties related to their field and expertise. It is also can be interpreted that teachers' competence is the ability of a teacher to do his main duties in accordance with his field of expertise. In this case, the main task of the teacher consists of the ability to design lesson plans, teaching in the class room, and evaluate student learning outcomes.

Rabo (2018) classified several characteristics of competent teachers such as a) having goals and intentions to develop students' thinking skills and effective nature. b) individualize and meet the individual needs of students. c) provide positive treatment to students and create a pleasant learning environment. d) love children and respect every child. e) professionalism and organization of daily work and use of time wisely. f) be responsible for their work, contribute to the school, parents, and society. g) has a good personality, show work ethic, humorous, and creative. h) responsive to change, showing initiative and positive attitude towards change. g) able to complete tasks on time if trusted. h) able to maintain the ethical purposes of the profession as a teacher, both in the school environment and in the community.

Zulfakar (2020) defines that the requirements to become a competent teacher: a) has a comprehensive knowledge base, have critical intellectuality, and work for the interests and progress of their students. b) can establish good relations with students and teach new things to students. c) able to create a conducive learning environment, an open environment that can encourage students to apply different learning models. d) act as a researcher in the field of education. Actively involved, have a critical attitude towards education, teaching, and learning, competent in conducting research, open to innovative ideas and approaches, enhance self-capacity and learning process. e) able to adapt in personal and group interactions. f) able to carry out activities in one theme or various other activities.

Teacher competence must be improved continuously to create the meaningful learning process and quality of the school graduates. The importance of teacher competence increased because it can be affected their values, behavior, communication, goals, and effective teaching practices (Parker, 2018). Mustikawati et al (2020) state that teacher competence can be improved through formal education, training, and teacher involvement in some teacher communities. Furthermore, Madjida (2020) teacher competence can also be increased through seminars, courses, and mentoring regularly. Continuing education to a higher level is the first step to improve teacher competence. Several research results reveal that continuing education to a higher level can increase teacher competence Egert et al (2020). Teacher competence can also be improved through regular training. The results of empirical studies show that attending training can improve teacher knowledge, teacher competence, and teacher performance outcomes (Slameto et al., 2017), (Qomariah, 2020), and (Pohan et al., 2021).

Online Training

One of the efforts that can be implemented to improve teacher competence is hold the training which regularly followed by teachers, in this case through online training. Hasan Basri, et al (2015) suggested that the training objectives consist of three, namely: a) Cognitive domain, which means that the purpose of the training is to increase the knowledge of the trainees. b) Affective domain, which means that the purpose of the training is to improve the behavior and character of teachers as trainees. c) Psychomotor domain, which means that the purpose of the training is to improve the skills of teachers in teaching. From the information above, it can be concluded that the purpose of the training is to increase the mastery of science according to the field, the attitudes and skills of the trainee teachers. Online training is the training which carried out in a network assisted by internet access services. Online training can be done through e-learning platforms, websites, word press, and other platforms. Online training is very useful for teachers to adopt specific skills needed in class to teach the students. After all, education should not be completely equal with training, and the role of professional teachers is to explain the educational process, and analyze it in relation to the reasons, and needs why certain learning experiences are beneficial. (Sue S., et al. 2020).

The results of previous empirical studies showed that the online and offline training have significant effect on increasing teacher competence. The results of the research by Pohan, et al (2021) showed that online training has successfully to improve the competence of teachers in the outer regions of Indonesia. Teachers could attend training flexibly without leaving the workplace and without high payment. This finding was in line with the research results of Mustikawati et al (2020) revealed that virtual training could improve teachers' competence in learning and increasing teachers' competence. The results of the research by Pratama et al (2020) virtual training also could improve the pedagogical competence of teachers, especially skills in teaching.

2. Research Method

The research method used in this research is the Mixed Method research method. The Mixed Method research method is a research method which combines quantitative and qualitative methods (Sugiyono, 2019). Furthermore, Creswell (2009) explains that combined research methods will be useful when quantitative methods or qualitative methods alone are not accurate enough to be used to understand research problems, or using qualitative and quantitative methods in combination will can get the best understanding (when compared to one method). The mixed method research model which applied in this study was a sequential exploratory model. The sequential exploratory model is a method that combines qualitative and quantitative research methods sequentially, where in the first stage it uses qualitative methods and in the second it uses quantitative methods (Sugiyono, 2019).

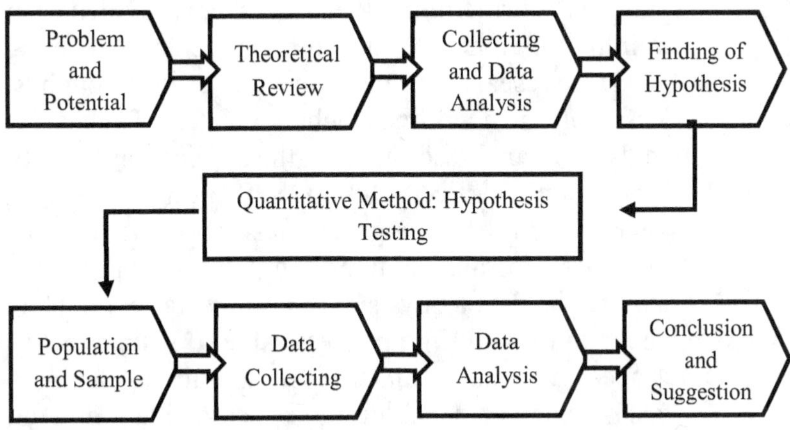

Figure 3.1 Sequential Exploratory Design (Sugiyono, 2019)

This research was conducted at the University of Riau Island, Batam City, at English Education Study Program in the fifth Semester of the 2020-2021 academic year. The informants of this study were the students of fifth semester, lecturers of English education study program, and head of the English education study program. In qualitative research, data collection activities, data analysis, and data credibility testing were carried out simultaneously in the field. Data collection was carried out through documentation studies and in-depth interviews and testing of research data was carried out using triangulation techniques. The data analyzed refers to the Miles & Huberman model which consists of data collection, data reduction, data display, and conclusion.

In quantitative research, the researcher used pre-experimental research method with a One-group pretest-posttest design. The subjects of this study were the fifth semester students of the English education study program with the total of 16 students. The first data collection technique was done through a pre-test, namely scoring the designing lesson plans and online teaching practices. Furthermore, the researchers provided online training for eight meetings through the zoom meeting platform. Next, the researcher gave a post-test exam through writing lesson plans and online teaching practice. The results of this study were analyzed by using the application of Statistical Product and Service Solution (SPSS) version 21 to determine the results of the homogeneity test, normality test, and hypothesis testing and to present the results in the form of tables. The data analysis of this study was explained if the post-test value (O2) > pre-test value (O1) then the hypothesis is accepted. This means that virtual training can improve teacher competence in designing lesson plans and online teaching practice.

3. Result and Discussion

Qualitative Result

The findings of qualitative research indicate that the competence of students participating in virtual training as teacher candidates was still low category. However, it has increased after participating in virtual training. As stated above, the competencies described in this study were the ability to teach student virtually, which consists of the competence to design the planning of the learning implementation and the competence to teach students virtually. The learning implementation plan was an arrangement and description of learning activities that should be applied in the learning process in the classroom (Pohan, 2020). The components of the learning implementation plan consist of basic competencies and indicators of mastery achievement, learning objectives, strategies and methods, teaching materials and sources, learning tools and media, learning activities consisting of opening, implementation, and closing, learning instruments consisting of attitude assessment , knowledge, and skills, and principal validation. However, based on the policy of Merdeka Belajar curriculum 2020 version, the learning implementation plan component only consists of 3 components, namely learning objectives, learning activities consisting of opening, implementation, and closing, learning instruments consisting of attitude, knowledge, and skill assessments. The type of lesson plan analyzed in this study was a lesson plan based on the policy of Merdeka Belajar curriculum 2020 version.

Online teaching competence is the ability of teachers to prepare relevant and applicable teaching materials, the competence to explain the lesson materials communicatively and involve students in the learning process actively with various strategies and learning methods, so that learning objectives can be achieved optimally. Online teaching competence required more practice and preparation compared to create the pleasant and normal learning situation. Competence can be developed through training process by experiencing it directly or by learning according to the individual characteristics of the teacher (Minh Gian, et al, 2021). Online teaching competencies consist of the ability to open learning, conduct learning that actively involves students, explain teaching materials effectively, master teaching materials, respond to student questions, provide feedback, create an interesting learning atmosphere, and be able to communicate well with students, and measuring student learning outcomes (Pohan, 2020).

Based on document studies, observations and interviews with virtual trainees, the findings of this qualitative research can be described. Firstly, the ability of virtual training participants in compiling online learning plans has not yet reached the standard indicated by an average score of 63.06. The training participants did not understand the essence of the lesson plan based on the policy of Merdeka Belajar curriculum 2020 version because this concept was still new and had not been studied. The curriculum studied in learning and learning lectures is the 2013 curriculum where these two curricula have many differences. The curriculum changing have given the impact that the teachers and prospective teachers not mastering the concepts and principles of planning the implementation of the curriculum. The trainees have difficulty in developing the steps of learning activities that will be applied in online learning

Secondly, the ability of the trainees in virtual teaching practice has not yet reached the standard of indicator. The low ability of virtual teaching practice was evidenced by the results of a document study where the average value of the trainees was 53.5. Through observation activities, it was found that the training participants had not mastered the operation of the online learning platform effectively. Online learning has not been implemented effectively because the implementation of learning does not reflect the activities arranged in the lesson plan. Students have not been actively guided to be involved in online learning. Another cause of ineffective online learning was internet network problems experienced by students. Students could not fully understand the material taught by them because the internet was disconnected. So that the learning outcomes have not run effectively. This finding was in line with the results research of Napitupulu (2020) where the students could not take online learning because of the low mastery of teacher technology. This finding was the main reason for continuing quantitative research by applying pre-experimental methods to overcome online learning problems faced by virtual trainees.

Quantitative Result

The results of the quantitative study were obtained from the results of the lesson plan assessment compiled by the trainees and the results of the online teaching ability assessment before and after participating in the virtual training. For more detailed information can be seen to the table 1 below.

Table 1. Result of Pre-Test dan Post-Test

Indicators	Result			
	Designing Lessong Plan		Online Teaching Competence	
	Pre-Test	Post-Test	Pre-Test	Post-Test
Total value	1009	1330	856	1259
Averge score	63.06	83.12	53.5	78.68
Highest score	83	90	70	84
Lowest score	50	75	20	86
Median	61	85	56	78
Modus	50	90	52	76

Table 1 above shows that the average value of the ability to prepare lesson plans before participating in virtual training is 63.06 and after participating in virtual training is 83.12. While the average value of online teaching skills before participating in the training was 53.5 and 78.68 after participating in the training. These results indicate that there is an increase in the competence of virtual training participants in preparing lesson plans by 20.06% and in the aspect of online teaching competence there is an increase of 25.18%..

Normality Testing

The normality test was carried out by using SPSS analysis using the One-Sample Kolmogorov-Simirnov Test. The decision making in this test is if the significance value (Sig.) were bigger than 0.05, the research data were normally distributed. Meanwhile, if the significance value (Sig.) were smaller than 0.05, the research data were not normally distributed. Below are the results of the One-Sample Kolmogorov-Simirnov Test for normality.

Table 2. One-Sample Kolmogorov-Smirnov Test

Designing Of Lesson Plan		Unstandard. Residual	Online Teaching Competence		Unstandard. Residual
N		16	N		16
Normal Parameters[a,b]	Mean	0E-7	Normal Parameters[a,b]	Mean	0E-7
	Std. Deviation	5.12782511		Std. Deviation	4.46657231
Most Extreme Differences	Absolute	.170	Most Extreme Differences	Absolute	.133
	Positive	.155		Positive	.133
	Negative	-.170		Negative	-.077
Kolmogorov-Smirnov Z		.679	Kolmogorov-Smirnov Z		.532
Asymp. Sig. (2-tailed)		.745	Asymp. Sig. (2-tailed)		.940

Based on table 2 above, it can be seen that the results of the normality test with the One-Sample Kolmogorov-Smirnov test can be described as normal. The table shows that the significance value for designing of lesson plan is $0.745 > 0.05$, and for online teaching competence is $0.940 > 0.05$ it can be concluded that the residual values are normally distributed.

Hypothesis Testing

This hypothesis test used the Paired Simple t-test to determine whether the application of virtual training could improve trainees' online teaching competence at University of Riau Kepulauan. The basic of decision making was if the significance value (2-tailed) < 0.05 then there was a significant difference between the pre-test and post-test scores. And if the significance value (2-tailed) > 0.05 then there was no significant difference between the pre-test and post-test scores. Below are the results of the hypothesis test.

Table 3. The Result of Hypothesis Testing by Paired Simple t-test

		Paired Differences					t	df	Sig. (2-tailed)
		Mean	Std. Deviation	Std. Error Mean	95% Confidence Interval of the Difference				
					Lower	Upper			
Pair 1	PretestLP - PosttestLP	-20.063	9.483	2.371	-25.116	-15.009	-8.462	15	.000
Pair 2	PretestTOC - PosttestTOC	-25.188	11.385	2.846	-31.254	-19.121	-8.849	15	.000

Based on the results of the hypothesis test in table 3 above, it can be seen that there is a significant difference between the pre-test and post-test scores both of trainees' competence in designing lesson plan and teaching online after participating in virtual training. This is indicated by the results of the Paired Simple t-test where the significance designing lesson plan value (2-tailed) is 0.00 < 0.05 and the significance online teaching competence value (2-tailed) is 0.00 < 0.05. In accordance with the basis for the conclusion above, it can be concluded that virtual training has given the effect on improving trainees' online teaching competence at University of Riau Kepulauan.

Discussion

This research was conducted in order to measure the effect of the virtual training to improve the students online teaching competence. The results of qualitative research indicate that the competence of students participating in virtual training as teacher candidates was still low category. However, it has increased after participating in virtual training. As stated above, the competencies described in this study were the teachers' competence in online teaching practice, which consists of the ability to prepare a learning implementation plan and the ability to teach the student in online. The learning implementation plan was an arrangement and description of learning activities that will be applied in the learning process in the classroom and in the practice room (Pohan, 2020). One of the competence of technician referred to the ability of preparing the lesson plan in accordance with the provisions of independent learning. The ability to arrange learning administration was a characteristic of professional teachers (Gutierez, 2020) and then applied it to improve student competence (Stemberger, 2020), and measured the results of student learning progress (De Simone, 2020).

The ability of students in preparing lesson plans increased after participating in virtual training. Through this virtual training, students were able to understand the structure and components of a lesson plan. Students were guided to develop learning objectives in the lesson plan based on Bloom's taxonomy. In the learning objectives, students were guided to develop goals to be achieved from the aspect of knowledge according to the teaching material, skills that must be mastered after participating in learning, and the internalization of national character values such as religious, nationalist, mutual cooperation, independent, and integrity characters. Furthermore, the training participants were guided to develop learning activities based on the syntax of learning strategies or learning methods to achieve the formulated learning objectives. Training participants were also guided to develop learning instruments to measure student learning outcomes which consist of aspects of attitudes, knowledge, and skills.

The ability to prepare lesson plans needs to be mastered by prospective teacher students because this work was one of the main obligations of teachers. The ability to develop lesson plans affects the effectiveness of learning in the teaching and learning process. Through lesson plans, teachers were required to know where the learning process started from, knowing what students must achieve in learning, knowing how to teach students so that students were able to achieve learning targets and objectives, knowing what strategies and methods should be used to achieve learning objectives, and knowing what to measure and what measuring instruments to use. Thus, the learning process will take place effectively where students can play an active role in the learning process. The success of students in achieving learning objectives could not be separated from the role of the teacher. For this reason, teachers must prepare for learning carefully before starting the learning process so that the learning process can take place effectively.

Teacher competence could be improved through several efforts, one of the proven efforts was through training. This was in line with teachers (Slameto et al., 2017), (Qomariah, 2020), and (Pohan et al., 2021) stated that teacher competence could be improved through regular training in order to improve teacher knowledge, teacher competence, outcomes, and teacher performance. In this virtual training, students were guided intensely on how to organize online learning by utilizing various online platforms. The trainees were trained how to open and close online classes in a communicative manner which consisted of several activities such as literacy activities, character development, and brain storming to focus students on learning. According to Sukirman (2012), opening and closing learning is an activity carried out in a structured manner in learning according to the plans drawn up in the lesson plan. Opening learning is the first effort that teachers must make in learning activities to create student preconditions so that students can focus and know what will be learned and what must be achieved in learning.

Students of Riau Islands University in the English Education Study Program as participants of this virtual training were trained to master class management skills well. Class management skills can be interpreted as teacher skills to create and optimalize the learning conditions (Pohan et al, 2020), both in face-to-face learning and online learning. Participants were repeatedly trained how to explain learning objectives and teaching materials effectively in online learning so that students could understand what the teacher explained. This was in line with Arikunto (2006) states that the purpose of classroom management is to discipline students so that students can follow the learning process with focus. Sharpen the ability and skills of asking students, building polite communication, and managing the class effectively so that students are actively involved in learning.

Particularly, the trainees were trained to improve skills in using online learning media, the ability to provide reinforcement and the ability to implement relevant learning methods. Mastering the use of media in online learning is important because the purpose of using media was to concrete concepts that are still abstract, for example by using pictures, schematics, graphs, and models so that students can more easily understand teaching materials. Optimalized of the using of learning media can improve the function of students' senses so that the weakness of one sense can be balanced with the strength of the other senses. Provided the skills for training participants how to provide reinforcement to students in the learning process. Reinforcement is a response to a behavior that can allow the repetition of that positive behavior (Pohan, et al, 2020). Through the provision of reinforcement, it can increase students' attention in learning, maintain motivation, and control students to encourage positive behavior.

The findings of qualitative research have provided a clear illustration of student competence in teaching online. The results of qualitative research were followed up with quantitative research with pre-experimental models to help solve problems faced by students at the Riau Islands University in the English Education Study Program. Based on the results of statistical analysis that the ability to prepare lesson plans and the ability to teach online increased where the significant value (2-tailed) was $0.00 < 0.05$. This means virtual training in the ability to compose lesson plans and the ability to teach online. There were several reasons virtual training could increase the students ability in designing of lesson plan and online teaching practice, such as collaboration among the students, flexibility of training time, face-to-face online communication and enthusiasm of training participants. This is in line with the results of research conducted by (Sue S., et al. 2020., Mustikawati, et al., 2020., & Pratama, et al., 2020).

4. Conclussions and Suggestions
4.1. Conclussions

Based on the above discussion, the results of this research can be concluded that the virtual training conducted by researchers can improve the students' competence in designing lesson plan by the value (2-tailed) is $0.00 < 0.05$ and the students' online teaching competence by the value (2-tailed) is $0.00 < 0.05$. In accordance with the basis for the conclusion above, it can be concluded that virtual training has given the effect on improving students' online teaching competence at Riau Islands University in the English Education Study Program.

4.2. Suggestions

Based on the research conclusions above, the researcher can provide suggestions to researchers, teachers, and school principals in order to:

1) Implementing the virtual training to improve the students' online teaching competence.
2) Conducting similar research with different or the same variables to improving students' online teaching competence.
3) Conducting the same research with different variables in other university to improve the students' online teaching competence.

4) Providing equitable training by virtual training to the students and teachers in improving the students and teachers' online teaching competence.

5) Follow up on the results and realization of virtual training continuously, evaluate, and reorganizing to ensure the effectiveness of the next virtual training in improving the students and teachers' online teaching competence.

References

Creswell, John. W. (2016). *Research Design: Pendekatan Metode Kualitatif, Kuantitatif, dan Campuran.* Edisi Keempat. Yogyakarta: Pustaka Belajar.

De Simone, J. J. (2020). The Roles of Collaborative Professional Development, Self-Efficacy, and Positive Affect in Encouraging Educator Data Use to Aid Student Learning, Teacher Development. *An International Journal of Teachers' Professional Development.* DOI: 10.1080/13664530.2020.1780302.

Egert, F., Dederer, V., & Fukkink, R. G. (2020). The Impact of In-Service Professional Development on the Quality of Teacher-Child Interactions in Early Education and Care: A Meta-Analysis. *Educational Research Review, (29), 100309.*

Gutierez, S. B. (2020). Collaborative Lesson Planning as a Positive 'Dissonance' to the Teachers' Individual Planning Practices: Characterizing the Features Through Reflections-On-Action, Teacher Development. *An International Journal of Teachers' Professional Development. DOI: 10.1080/13664530.2020.1856177.*

Hasan Basri & Rusdiana. (2015) *Manajemen Pendidikan dan Pelatihan.* Bandung: Pustaka Setia, 2015, h. 103

Jacob, O. N., Deborah, J., Elizabeth, A., & Samuel, A. (2021). Impact of Covid-19 on Educational Planning in Federal Capital Territory, Abuja, Nigeria. *Educational Journal of History and Humanities, Volume 4 (1), 55-62.*

Madjida, A., Suudb, F. M., & Bahiroh, S. (2020). Teacher Competence, Commitment and Work Motivation: What Influences Performance in Yogyakarta. *International Journal of Innovation, Creativity and Change, Volume 13(11), 135-147.*

Miles, M. B, Huberman, A. M, dan Saldana, J. (2014). *Qualitative Data Analysis, A Methods Sourcebook.* Edition 3. USA: Sage Publications. Terjemahan Tjetjep Rohindi Rohidi, UI-Press.

Minh Gian, P & Dặng Quoc Bao. (2021). The Competences of Teaching Staff and Principals in the Context of Educational Innovation and School Development. *International Education Studies, Volume 14(1), 65-75.*

Mursalin., Sarkadi., & Hidayat, D. R. (2021). Preparation of Basic School Teachers in Online Teaching in the Pandemic Time Covid-19. *International Journal of Multicultural and Multireligious Understanding, Volume 8(5), 637-644.*

Mustikawati, E & Qomariah, N. (2020). The Effect of Education, Training and Competency on Teacher Performance. *International Journal of Business and Management Invention, Volume 9(10), 14-20.*

Mseleku, Z. (2020). A Literature Review of E-Learning and E-Teaching in the Era of Covid-19 Pandemic. *International Journal of Innovative Science and Research Technology, Volume 5(10), October-2020, 588-596.*

Napitupulu, R. M. (2020). Dampak Pandemi Covid-19 Terhadap Kepuasan Pembelajaran Jarak Jauh. *Jurnal Inovasi Teknologi Pendidikan, Volume 1(1), 23-33.*

Nic Beech & Anseel, F. (2020). Covid-19 and Its Impact On Management Research and Education: Threats, Opportunities, and a Manifesto. *British Journal of Management, Vol. 31, 447-449.*

Parker, L. (2018). Teacher Competencies or Certification Competencies. *Journal of Behavioral Disorders, Volume 5(3), 163-168.*

Pohan, A. E., Daulay, H. M., & Sahrir, A. (2021). Improving Teachers' Professionalism Through Blended-Based Training in Indonesia's Remote Area. *London Journal of Social Science, Volume 1(1), 67-78.*

Pohan, A. E. (2020). *Konsep Pembelajaran Dalam Jaringan Berbasis Pendekatan Ilmiah (Scientific Approach).* Purwodadi: CV. Sarnu Untung

Pohan, A. E., Yulia, D & Husna, A. (2020). *Micro Teaching Based On Scientific Approach.* Indra Mayu. CV. Penerbit Adab.

Pratama, L. D & Lestari, W. (2020). Pengaruh Pelatihan Terhadap Kompetensi Pedagogik Guru Matematika. *Jurnal Cendekia, Volume 4(1), 278-285.*

Rabo, U. M. (2018). Relationship Between Teacher Competence, School Climate and Academic Performance of Public Senior Secondary School Students in Sokoto State, Nigeria. *International Journal of Humanities and Social Science Invention, Volume 7(11), 34-40.*

Siri, A., Supartha I. W. G., Sukaatmadja, I. P. G., & Rahyuda, A. G. (2020). Does Teacher Competence and Commitment Improve Teacher's Professionalism. *Cogent Business and Management, Volume 7(1), 1-13.*

Slameto, Sulasmono, B. S., & Wardani, K. W. (2017). Peningkatan Kinerja Guru Melalui Pelatihan Beserta Faktor Penentunya. *Jurnal Pendidikan Ilmu Sosial, Volume 27(2), 38-47.*

Stemberger, T. (2020). The Teacher Career Cycle and Initial Motivation: The Case of Slovenian Secondary School Teachers, Teacher Development. *An International Journal of Teachers' Professional Development.* 24(5), 709-726.

Sue Swaffield & Philip E. Poekert. (2020). Leadership for Professional Learning, Special Issue. *Journal Professional Development in Education, Volume 46(4), 517-520.*

Sukirman, D. (2012). *Micro Teaching*. Jakarta. Ditjen Kemenag

Sunyoto, D. (2015). *Penelitian Sumber Daya Manusia*. PT. Buku Seru Unggul

Tarkar, P. (2020). Impact Of Covid-19 Pandemic On Education System. *International Journal of Advanced Science and Technology, Volume 29(9), 3812-3814.*

Zulfakar. (2020). Continuous Education For All. *International Journal of Multicultural and Multireligious Understanding, 7(7), 297-307. http://dx.doi.org/10.18415.ijmmu.v7i7.1853*

Zulfakar. (2019). Educational Research Methods in Qualitative and Quantitative Perspectives. *International Journal of Multidisciplinary and Current Research, Vol.7 July-Aug, 429-437.*

London International Conferences

londonic.uk   ukeyconsultingpublishing.co.uk

Communication Strategies Used by Students of English Conversation Club of Sragen Bilingual Boarding School

Begench Soyunov
Sebelas Maret University

Abstract

This study was aimed to find out the types of communication strategies used by the learners of Sragen, Bilingual Boarding School Sragen (SBBS) year X and to figure out the most types used by the learners. The subject of the study was 20 members of English Conversation Club Students (ECC) of Sragen, Bilingual Boarding School Sragen Year X. The interview was conducted in this research. The interview was used to help the researcher set the classroom with debate classroom, recorded, and then transcripted the conversation.

The researcher, adopted Qualitative Research which requires. The result of the study shows that there are eleven types of communication strategies used by the learners; circumlocution, approximation, word coinage, code switching, use of nonlinguistic means, appeal for help, use of all purpose words, using fillers, using wrong terms, self correction, and repetition. Fillers, Circumlocution and Repetition are the strategies mostly used by the learners. Based on the result of the study, the researcher inferred that the learners of SBBS some difficulties in their communication. The higher number of students using fillers, indicates that they hesitate too much in delivering their opinion. They are also nervous, afraid to make mistakes, and not confident enough to give their opinion.

After analyzing the data, researcher found out that the chance in communication strategies in class was seen clearly and all the responses from the students were positive. It can be indicated that there was an improvement in students' conversation. Moreover, the communication strategies of students are good.

Summarizing the abstract, from this research the researcher has learned that communication strategies of SBBS students are very good and has the knowledge of English above the average. Because SBBS's students learn all lesson in English and can be speak in English very well. There are also some students that have attended international Olympiads and they got golden, silver and bronze medals. Moreover, teachers also have good skill to manage the class, creating better ambiance for students to learn English. Therefore, most of the lessons were very joyful with active and courage students.

Keywords: Communication, Communication Strategies, Type of Communication Strategies, Qualitative Research

Digital transformation with the Pandemic Era

Mehmet Ali Eroğlu
ITACon Academy
dr@emali.org

Abstract

The ongoing pandemic has torn us apart especially when the infection is found first. It had affected the physical human interactions dramatically, forced people to digital transformation and made an effect on the numbers of physical communications on business, family, healthcare and education. The presentation that will be presented focuses on the digitalization of the communications between people during the pandemic. I will be mentioning digitization on business; the increasing amount of social media usage, education; the relations between students and teachers plus the platforms that are used for continuing education, health; the relations between patient and doctor plus the advantages of online appointment. The digital transformation got easier after a lot of people started using it and got more eligible for people from everywhere and every age. It made it easier to ensure the transformation while following the instructions step by step. The transformation to the digital world has been the obligation in order to continue working, educating, providing healthcare, social activities and much more interaction types. It had become an essential part of everybody since the beginning of the pandemic period. The invention and popularization of computers and phones resulted in the constant increase of digitization and digital transformation in the early 2000s. Nevertheless, the irremissible pandemic accelerated the speed of the transformation and made it possible to be reached from every place and person.

Keywords: Digital transformation, pandemic, digitization

London International Conferences

londonic.uk   ukeyconsultingpublishing.co.uk

Traditional Games as Fun Media in Strengthening Multiple Intelligences During Learning at Home in the Corona Pandemic

Elsa Putri Ermisah Syafril
University of PGRI Yogyakarta
elsaputri.es@gmail.com

Abstract

The corona pandemic is not over yet. Currently, Indonesia is implementing social activity restrictions in several areas since last July 2021. It causes everyone just stay at home and do the activities from home, including the learning process. Of course, it causes every student feels bored and become stress because basically, the students in childhood need social interaction and excitement, like playing. Actually, there are many Indonesian traditional games that can be played at home with the family. However, based on data, there are about 40% of Indonesian traditional games have become extinct and about 65% of Indonesian children are no longer familiar with traditional games. Therefore, this study aims to: 1) explain the conditions of learning at home during the pandemic; 2) explain the application of traditional games can stimulate learning and social interaction activities at home; 3) explain the existence of traditional games as fun learning media for strengthening personal character as well as increasing multiple intelligences.

A qualitative design is used in this study. Then, a critical paradigm to find new concept from local knowledge with indigenous ethnography approach is also used in this study. The data is collected by the techniques of observation (some using students' video from other places while playing traditional games), interviews, documentation, and the study of documents. Moreover, some students from several places in Indonesia become informants of this research (25 students from elementary school and junior high school). Meanwhile, the collected data are analyzed using the interactive model analysis by Miles and Huberman (focus on descriptive, emotion, and values coding). The results of this study are: (1) the condition of learning process at home during pandemic experienced many obstacles that make students bored and stressed; (2) the application of traditional games can stimulate learning and social interaction activities at home; and (3) the existence of traditional games as fun learning media for strengthening personal character as well as increasing multiple intelligences.

Keywords: Traditional game, Multiple intelligences, Learning at home, Corona pandemic

1. The Background

The corona pandemic is not over yet. As of Thursday (July 1, 2021), the daily case in Indonesia reached 24,836 cases and mortality rate increased by 250% in the same period [1]. Because of this condition, Indonesia is implementing social activity restrictions in several areas since last July 2021. This effort is through the COVID-19 Handling Task Force with Circular (SE) No. 16 of 2021 concerning Travel of Domestic People during the COVID-19 Pandemic Period, which is effective from 26 July 2021. In line with that, the Ministry of Law and Human Rights also issued regulation (Permenkumham) No. 27 of 2021 concerning Restrictions on Foreigners Entering Indonesia During the Emergency PPKM Period. It is enforced to prevent the entry of virus variants originating from outside Indonesia [2]. This condition causes everyone just stay at home and do the activities from home, including the learning process. Of course, it causes every student feels bored and becomes stress because basically, the students in childhood need social interaction and excitement, like playing.

Actually, Indonesia has many traditional games that can be played at home with the family members. There are about 2500 traditional games in Indonesia (MZ. Alif in Gatra.com, 2018) [3]. However, based on data, there are about 40% of Indonesian traditional games have become extinct [4] and about 65% of Indonesian children are no longer familiar with traditional games [5]. Based on initial observations, there are several games that can increase students' knowledge about the diversity of Indonesian culture, especially Indonesian traditional games. In addition, these games can also stimulate students' multiple intelligences, and motivate students to keep studying even at home. The games are *engklek, congklak, cublak-cublak suweng, bentengan, ular naga, petak umpet,* and *ABC 5 Dasar.*

Based on previous scholar's research, traditional games are said being able to develop the moral and language aspects of students at school (Haris and Hastuti, 2016) [6]. Furthermore, the use of *engklek* in the learning process at school is able to strengthen students' mathematical abilities (Utami, 2018) [7] while preserving traditional games. Besides *engklek, congklak* can also improve the mathematical abilities of students at school (Muslihatun, et al., 2019) [8]. Then, *cublak-cublak suweng* contains many values of local wisdom that can shape the character of students (Kurniasari and Rahardi, 2019) [9]. Informatively, *bentengan* is a game that is included in the category of Indonesian intangible cultural heritage set by the Indonesian Ministry of Education and Culture in 2018 [10]. Meanwhile, the game of *ular naga* and *petak umpet* is considered beneficial for the physical development of early childhood (Pramudyani, 2020) [11] [12]. Finally, the game of *ABC 5 Dasar* is able to improve the ability of students' memorizing new vocabulary at school (Faizin, 2020) [13]. These studies focus on learning at school, not at home.

**Figure 1. Traditional Game *Bentengan*
(Intangible Cultural Heritage on 2018)**

Anthropologically, traditional games are part of local knowledge. Local knowledge (spirituality, values, thoughts, tastes, and body) begins and returns to the environment (Syafril, 2020) [14]. It means that traditional games start from knowledge with a background of environmental conditions and return to the surrounding environment, such as the game *congklak* which is made from wood and seeds or shells. This knowledge is obtained through experience and concrete understanding of the environment (Syafril, 2021) [15]. It is in line with experiential learning developed by Kolb: abstract conceptualization and concrete experience (understanding experience) as well as active experimentation and reflective observation (changing experience) (Kolb, 1984) [16]. This allows students (children) to be interested in learning and it becomes the stimulation of learning. In simpler terms, experiential learning includes abstract conceptualization, concrete experience, active experimentation, and reflective observation (Syafril, 2021) [17]. All of these things can be found by the students (children) in traditional games.

The traditional games mentioned above, are theoretically associated with learning aimed at increasing students' (children's) multiple intelligences. There are 8 categories of multiple intelligences introduced by Gardner, namely: naturalist, spatial, musical, logical reasoning (mathematical), interpersonal, body kinesthetic, linguistic, and intrapersonal intelligence (Amstrong, 2009; Gardner, 2006; and Gardner, 1993) [18] [19] [20]. In addition, traditional games are also examined from their function to strengthen the relationship between parents and children at home. Parent-child relationships have powerful effects on children's emotional well-being (Dawson & Ashman, 2000) [21].

Based on the background above, this study aims to: 1) explain the conditions of learning at home during the pandemic; 2) explain the application of traditional games can stimulate learning and social interaction activities at home; 3) explain the existence of traditional games as fun learning media for strengthening personal character as well as increasing multiple intelligences.

2. Method

This study uses a qualitative design and with a critical paradigm to find new concept from local knowledge with indigenous ethnography approach. The phenomenological approach used for collecting data about the phenomena of using traditional games and its function for strengthening multiple intelligences. It originates from philosophical and psychological knowledge based on the researcher's experience of a phenomenon in an area. In terms of the character of the data obtained, this approach is more dominated by interview techniques (Creswell & Creswell, 2018) [22].

This study also examines cultural and local wisdom of traditional games for strengthening multiple intelligences and children's character. So, this study also uses an ethnographic approach. The ethnographic approach is based on anthropological and sociological studies that examine the conditions of behavior, language, and actions that take place in a cultural group naturally for a long time (Creswell & Creswell, 2018) [22].

The data is collected by the techniques of observation (some using students' video from other places while playing traditional games), interviews, documentation, and the study of documents. Some students from several places in Indonesia become informants (25 students from elementary school and junior high school). Then, the collected data are analyzed using the interactive model analysis by Miles and Huberman (focus on descriptive, emotion, and values coding) (Miles, Huberman, and Saldana, 2014) [23].

For measuring the validity of the data, it is used triangulation techniques (sources), member checks (asking the same questions to different informants) and increasing observation persistence. This is in line with the data analysis technique used, namely an interactive model of data analysis that allows the researcher (as the main instrument) to measure data validity.

3. Discussion

As said in the background, the corona pandemic is not over yet that causes everyone just stay at home and do the activities from home, including the learning process. Of course, it causes every student feels bored and becomes stress.

The Conditions of Learning at Home During the Pandemic

There are many obstacles during learning at home. This condition dues to many things, such as the sudden pandemic condition and the problem of poor internet network. In addition, the use of online media makes the interactions between teachers and students are difficult so that it needs alternative media for attracting the students. Besides the difficulties faced by teachers, learning during the corona pandemic has also causes several problems for students, such as not all students have ICT devices for learning, such as cellphones and laptops (sometimes they have to alternate with parents and other relatives) and the understanding of students in using the media and learning the material. Learning from home also causes difficulties for the mentoring of parents while learning using online media because some parents work (from home too). Then, learning from home also affects the social interaction of students to others, and so many others. This is as conveyed by the following students:

(a) *"Saya kesulitan konsentrasi kalau belajar dari rumah karena penjelasan guru kadang-kadang tidak jelas."*
("I become difficult to concentrate when learning from home because the teacher's explanations are sometimes not clear.")

(b) *"Kalau belajar dari rumah, saya suka kangen teman-teman trus tidak bisa main. Bosan."*

("When I learn from home, I like to miss my friends and can't play together. Bored.")

Those make students become lazy, bored, and often stressed in facing learning without direct interaction with teachers and other friends. The condition can be seen from the data about Indonesia children during Corona pandemic: 47% feel bored at home; 35% worried about missing lessons; 20% miss their friends; 15% feel insecure; and 10% worried about the family's economic condition (BNPB, 2020) [24]. Then, from 25 informants of this research: 56% feel bored at home; 20% stress; 16% feel bored and stress; and 8% no answer (Elsa, 2021).

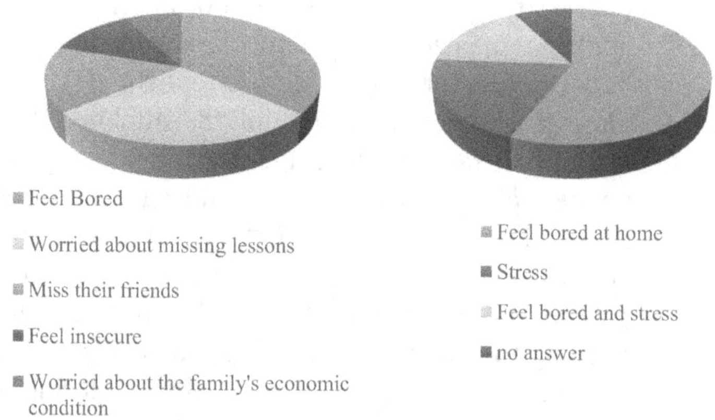

Figure 2. Diagram of Indonesian Children during Corona

Figure 3. Diagram of Indonesian Children during Corona (Informants)

From the diagram above, it can be seen that most students feel bored, anxious about missing their lessons because they can't understand the material while learning using online media, and feel stressed while learning at home. This if left unchecked can affect the psychological condition of students and cause them to be lazy or even not want to learn at all.

The Application of Traditional Games Stimulates Learning as Experiential Learning and Interaction Activities at Home

Indonesian society is a multicultural society which grows with a variety of cultural structures. Indonesian has many Indonesian traditional games that can be played at home with the family. It is about 2500 traditional games. Actually, many traditional games can be used as learning media for students (children) while at home.

As explained in the background of this research, learning by applicating the traditional game media is in line with experiential learning developed by Kolb (1984). The concept of experiential learning is abstract conceptualization and concrete experience (understanding experience) as well as active experimentation and reflective observation (changing experience) which make students (children) being interested in learning and it becomes the stimulation of learning. The students (children) experience the concrete condition for themselves how to count using *congklak* seeds or sing through the game *cublak cublak suweng* or also memorize vocabulary by playing *ABC 5 Dasar*. It becomes active experimentation for the students (children) in learning while playing as the following student opinions:

(c)*"Main congklak dengan kakak, aku jadi belajar berhitung dari bijinya. Trus, kalau main ABC 5 Dasar, aku belajar kata-kata baru. Asyik pokoknya."*
("When I play *congklak* with my sister, I learn how to count by using the seeds. Then, when I play *ABC 5 Dasar*, I learn new words. It's fun anyway.")

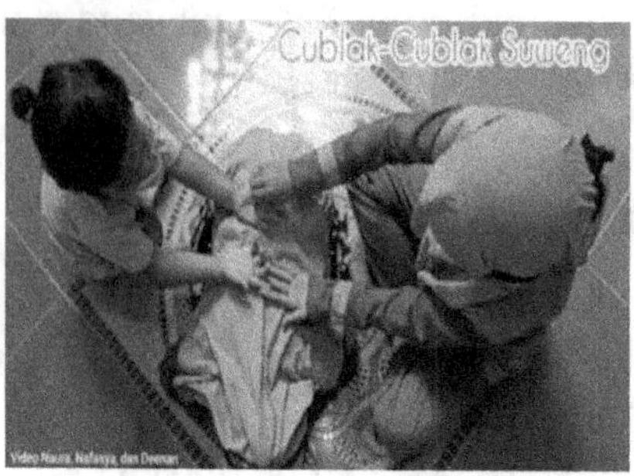

Figure 4. Traditional Game
Cublak Cublak Suweng

Figure 5. Traditional Game
ABC 5 Dasar with Family
Members

Besides being a stimulus through experiential learning, the use of traditional games can also be an interaction activity at home that can strengthen relationships between family members, especially parents and children. A good parent-child relationship can greatly affect a child's emotional condition, as stated by the following informants:

(d)"*Bermain mainan tradisional bersama keluarga selama di rumah membuat aku senang, tidak bosan, dan jadi lebih dekat dengan Ibu sama Bapak juga kakak.*"
("Playing traditional games with my family while at home makes me happy, not bored, and closer to my mother, father, and brother.")

Like the previous explanation, playing together between family members at home provides space for family members to "chat together", laugh, and have fun together. It can bring the relationship between family members closer. When the relationship between family members is getting closer, it makes students (children) comfortable at home which in the end makes them active and not lazy, especially when studying.

The Existence of Traditional Games as Fun Learning Media for Strengthening and Increasing Multiple Intelligences

a. *Engklek* and *Congklak*

Engklek; the game that is played on a playing field (can be on the floor, street, field, or other flat place) by two or more people (children). The players need pictures in the form of boxes and *gajo* (objects that are thrown while playing as a marker for the player's place). Then, the player should jump one foot on the boxes that have been made. This *engklek* game creates a sense of joy, trains the motoric development of students (children), honesty (intrapersonal), sportsmanship (interpersonal), and strengthens closeness with family members.

Figure 6. Traditional Game   Figure 7. Traditional Game
Engklek   *Congklak*

Congklak using *congklak* board with 7 holes and seeds which also amount to 7 for each hole. This game is played by 2 people who take turns if the seeds stop in an empty place. The player will be deemed to have won if the main hole is filled with more seeds. This game creates a sense of pleasure, increases the mathematical ability (thinking logically) of students (children) when playing *congklak* seeds, respect for others, honesty (intrapersonal), sportsmanship (interpersonal), and strengthens closeness with family members. As stated by the following informant:

(e)"*Saat bermain congklak, aku senang dan aku bisa belajar menjumlahkan dan mengurang dari biji congklaknya. Aku juga senang karena Ibu juga main sama aku.*"

("When playing congklak, I'm happy and I can learn to add and subtract from the congklak seeds. I'm also happy because my mother is playing with me too.")

b. *Cublak-Cublak Suweng* and *Ular Naga*

Cublak-cublak suweng played by several students (children) while singing the song *'Cublak-cublak Suweng'*. One player bends down on the floor, using her/his back as a 'table'. Other players place an open palm on the back of a bent student (child). While singing, one person moves a seed or small object from one palm to the next until the song ends. The rotated object is held by the child who received it when the song ended. All players keep their palms closed and the one who bends down has to guess in which hand the object is hidden.

In value, the song *Cublak-cublak Suweng* means that if you are looking for treasure, don't follow your lust but return to a clean conscience so that it will be easier to find happiness, and don't get lost in the path that forgets the afterlife. The song *Cublak-cublak Suweng* is a cultural heritage originating from *Walisongo*, who spread Islam on the Java which contains moral values about the attitude that humans should do. Thus, this game creates a sense of joy, teaches good moral values, Indonesian culture (Javanese), musical ability (singing), respect for others, honesty (intrapersonal), sportsmanship (interpersonal), and strengthens closeness with family members.

Ular naga; a game that can be played by many people while singing " *ular naga panjangnya bukan kepalang, menjalar-jalar selalu riang-kemari. Umpan yang lezat itulah yang dicari, ini dianya yang terperangkap*" (the dragon's length is absurdly long, always creeping around cheerfully here and there. That delicious bait is what you're looking for, this is what's caught in the trap). Two players become the gate, one person becomes the mother of dragon and the rest become the children of the dragon. The game begins when the mother dragon and her cubs circle through the gates while singing. When the song ends, the two gates will be lowered while catching the dragon child and offer to choose which gate to follow, and so on. The new mother dragon is selected from the gate with the most offspring. This game creates a sense of joy, musical ability (singing), honesty (intrapersonal), sportsmanship (interpersonal), and strengthens closeness with family members, as stated by the following informants:

(f) "*Main cublak-cublak suweng sama ular naga ada nyanyinya, aku senang. Aku juga senang karena semua keluarga mau main.*"

("Playing *cublak-cublak suweng* with dragon snakes has singing, I'm happy. I'm also happy because the whole family wants to play.")

Figure 8. Traditional Game *Ular Naga*

c. *Petak Umpet* and *Bentengan*

Petak umpet (hide and seek) is a kind of search and hide game that can be played by 2 or more people which is generally done outdoors. But during a pandemic, it can be done at home. This game creates a sense of joy, trains motoric development of students (children), honesty (intrapersonal), sportsmanship (interpersonal), and strengthens closeness with family members.

Bentengan is the game played by two groups which consisting of 4 to 8 people. Each group chooses a place as a base, usually a pillar or rock as a *benteng* (fort). The main objective of the game is to attack and take over the opponent's 'fort' by touching the pole or pillar that the opponent has chosen and shouting the word "*benteng*". This game creates a sense of pleasure, trains motoric development of students (children), the attitude cooperation, honesty (intrapersonal), sportsmanship (interpersonal), and strengthens closeness with family members.

d. *ABC 5 Dasar*

The game of *ABC 5 Dasar* was a very popular game in the 1990s. This game is very easy to play because it does not require any tools, only fingers and educative. When playing, students (children) can sit in a circle facing each other, then make game rules and what categories will be played, for example the category of animal names. Next, all players say the *ABC 5 Dasar* while pointing out how many fingers they want. The finger is calculated in alphabetical order to determine the letter that will be the basis for guessing on the last finger. For example, on the last finger is the letter R, then all players find all kinds of animals with the first letter R, such as *rusa* (deer), *rubah* (fox), and others. Players who cannot pronounce the correct vocabulary will receive consequences according to the agreement. This game creates a sense of joy, improves verbal skills and increases the vocabulary of students (children) (linguistic abilities), trains concentration, honesty (intrapersonal), sportsmanship (interpersonal), and strengthens closeness with family members.

(g)"*Main ABC 5 Dasar dengan kakak dan Bapak sangat menyenangkan. Aku jadi tau banyak kata-kata, termasuk aku juga jadi belajar kata-kata bahasa Inggris.*"

("Playing ABC 5 Dasar with my brother and father is so much fun. I got to know a lot of words, including I also learned English words.")

Based on the explanation above, some of Indonesian traditional games can be played at home during pandemic. Then, Indonesian traditional games become fun media for learning at home and make closed relationship between family members. Traditional games also can strengthen personal character and multiple intelligences.

4. Conclusions and Suggestion

Conclusions

The conditions of learning at home during the pandemic has many obstacles that make students become lazy, bored, and often stressed in facing learning without direct interaction with teachers and other friends.

The application of traditional games stimulates learning and social interaction activities at home, gives new experiential learning, and builds closed emotional relationship between family members.

The existence of traditional games as fun learning media for strengthening personal character (the attitude cooperation, sportsmanship, respect for others, honest, etc.) and increasing multiple intelligences (based on traditional games), especially: (a) getting to know Indonesian culture; (b) teaching character education; (c) practicing intrapersonal and interpersonal skills; (d) stimulating fine motoric skills; (e) improving musical skills; (f) practicing verbal/linguistic skills; and (g) honing math skills.

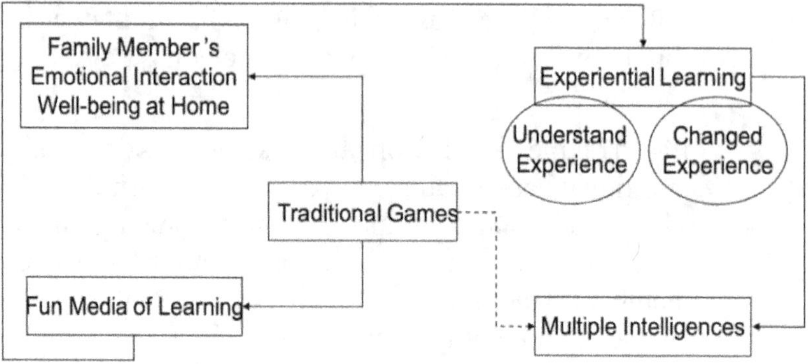

Figure 9. Traditional Games as Fun Media of Learning at Home

Suggestion

Every traditional game in other places in Indonesia or other
countries can be researched and adopted as an media to
strengthen personal character and multiple intelligences during
and post-pandemic.

References

[1] https://www.bbc.com/indonesia/dunia-57675990 (accessed on July 01, 2021).

[2] https://covid19.go.id/p/berita/pemerintah-perkuat-penanganan-covid-19-dalam-masa-ppkm-level-1-4 (accessed on July 27, 2021).

[3] https://www.gatra.com/detail/news/310956-Zaini-Alif-:-Bapak-Permainan-Tradisional-Pendiri-Komunitas-Hong (accessed on June 27, 2021).

[4] https://news.detik.com/internasional/d-3087069/melalui-komunitas-hong-zaini-alif-lestarikan-permainan-tradisional (accessed on June 30, 2021).

[5] https://www.antaranews.com/berita/630441/kebanyakan-anak-indonesia-lupa-permainan-tradisional (accessed on June 30, 2021).

[6] Haris, Irfan dan Dwi Hastuti. "Pemanfaatan Permainan Tradisional sebagai Media Pembelajaran Anak Usia Dini untuk Mengembangkan Aspek Moral dan Bahasa Anak". *Eksplorasi: JurnalIlmu Sosial dan Humaniora*. Vol. 28. No.2. Februari 2016.

[7] Utami, Nur Isnaini. "Engklek Geometri: Upaya Pelestarian Permainan Tradisional Melalui Proses Pembelajaran Matematika di SMP Muhammadiyah 4 Surabaya". *J-ADIMAS (Jurnal Pengabdian kepada Masyarakat)*. Vol. 6, No. 1. Juli 2018: 12 – 18.

[8] Muslihatun, A., et al. "Pemanfaatan Permainan Tradisional Untuk Media Pembelajaran: Congklak Bilangan Sebagai Inovasi Pembelajaran Matematika Sekolah Dasar". *Transformasi: Jurnal Pengabdian Masyarakat*. Vol. 15. No. 1. 2019: 14-22.

[9] Kurniasari, Yohana Rina dan R. Kunjana Rahardi. "Nilai - Nilai Kearifan Lokal dalam Permainan Tradisional *Cublak -*

Cublak Suweng di Yogyakarta: Kajian Ekolinguistik". *Jurnal Pendidikan Bahasa dan Sastra Indonesia*. Vol. 8. No. 2. 2019.

[10] https://warisanbudaya.kemdikbud.go.id/?newdetail&detailCatat=8939 (accessed on July 27, 2021).

[11] Pramudyani, Avanti Vera Risti. "Traditional Game of Ular Naga for Early Childhood Development from Teacher's Perspective". *Aulad Journal on Early Childhood*. Vol. 3. No. 1. April 2020: 8-13.

[12] https://icando.co.id/artikel/permainan-petak-umpet (accessed on June 03, 2021).

[13] Faizin, Khoirul. 2020. "Permainan "ABC 5 Dasar" untuk Meningkatkan Penguasaan Kosakata Bahasa Arab". *Muróbbî: Jurnal Ilmu Pendidikan*. Vol. 4, No. 1. Maret 2020.

[14] Syafril, Elsa Putri E. "Coronathropology; Local Wisdom During and After the Plague." *Malay Local Wisdom in the Period and After the Plague*: 17.

[15] Syafril, E. P. E., and W. Kurniawati. "PPT-Audio; The Alternative Audio-Visual Media for Online Learning during the Corona Pandemic." *Journal of Physics: Conference Series*. Vol. 1823. No. 1. IOP Publishing, 2021.

[16] Kolb, D.A. 1984. *Experiential Learning: Experience as The Source of Learning and Development*. New Jersey: Prentice-Hall.

[17] Syafri, Elsa Putri Ermisah, and Umi Kulsum. "TikTok; Media Pembelajaran Alternatif dan Atraktif pada Pelajaran PPKn Selama Pandemi di SMP Negeri 2 Mertoyudan." *Seri Prosiding Seminar Nasional Dinamika Informatika*. Vol. 5. No. 1. 2021.

[18] Amstrong, Thomas. 2009. *Multiple Intelligences in The Classroom, 3rd Edition*. Alexandria, Virginia USA: ASCD Member Books.

[19] Gardner, Howard. 2006. *Multiple Intelligences: New Horizons*. New York: Basic Books, *A Member of the Perseus Books Group*.

[20] Gardner, Howard. 1993. *Frames of Mind: The Theory of Multiple Intelligences*. New York: Basic Books, *A Member of the Perseus Books Group*.

[21] Dawson, G., & Ashman, S. B. "On the Origins of a Vulnerability to Depression: The Influence of The Early Social Environment on The Development of Psychobio-Logical Systems Related to Risk for Affective Disorder" in *The Effects of Adversity on Neurobehavioral Development. Minnesota Symposia on Child Psychology*. Vol. 31. 2000: 245–278. Mahwah, NJ: Lawrence Erlbaum and Associates.

[22] Creswell, John W. & J. David Creswell. 2018. *Research Design: Qualitative, Quantitative, and Mixed Methods Approaches, Fifth Edition*. Los Angeles: SAGE Publications, Inc.

[23] Miles, Matthew B., A. Michael Huberman, & Johnny Saldana. 2014. *Qualitative Data Analysis, Third Edition*. USA: SAGE Publications, Inc.

[24] https://edukasi.kompas.com/read/2020/11/13/162554571/47-persen-anak-indonesia-bosan-di-rumah-akademisi-ipb-beri-saran?page=all (accessed on May 31, 2021).

Artificial Intelligence and Machine Learning Applications in Education

Akif Celepcikay
Fort Bend ISD
akiftx@gmail.com

Yetkin Yildirim
Rice University
yetkin@rice.edu

Abstract

Artificial Intelligence (AI), Data Analytics, and Machine Learning technologies are poised to transform the field of education as we know it. They have already upended industries from retail to manufacturing and now that the coronavirus pandemic has accelerated the shift to online classrooms, with remote teacher-student interaction and remote curriculum test, AI-powered tools are more critical for teachers and students than ever before. AI-powered intelligent tutoring systems, AI chatbots can interact with students to increase engagement of students in studies, and Machine Learning algorithms can analyze student data. Together these provide great opportunities for improving student learning, will help teachers also and will also help in many other aspects of education. This chapter will highlight some of the most interesting real-world applications of AI and Machine Learning and explain the methodology of their implementation, then describe how they can improve student learning and the effectiveness of education systems. This chapter will also discuss the critical challenges that educators and researchers face when applying these technologies in the field of education. Finally, the chapter is concluded with a discussion of the roles AI and Machine Learning can play in post-pandemic education world and of promising technologies that could be significant driving forces for even more AI and Machine Learning applications in education in the future.

Keywords: artificial intelligence, machine learning, data analytics, intelligent tutoring systems, chatbots, learning management systems, algorithms, student modeling, personalized learning, online education, remote learning, technology in education, AI ethics in education

1. Introduction to Artificial Intelligence and Machine Learning

Before the discussion of the applications of AI and Machine Learning in education in details, it is imperative to clearly define and explain what AI and Machine Learning are, highlight the basic concepts and point to the main differences especially since the two terms have been used interchangeably even though they are different concepts.

Artificial Intelligence can be roughly stated as machines trying to understand the behavior patterns of humans and trying to mimic the behaviors such that it can replicate these actions. Artificial Intelligence has come into existence in 1956 with a group of people under John McCarthy and Alan Turing. The concept of AI is to learn from the experience based on a set of internal rules and conditions, which provide responses that are processed using huge amount of data. The purpose of AI is to solve the problems. Artificial intelligence enables computers to think at various stages and is a broad spectrum where it covers Machine Learning and Deep learning. It senses the data, reads, and finds reasons to act as per the situations and adapts to the situation.

Machine Learning came into existence in 1980's where it borrowed the concepts and methods of models that belong to statistics and probability. Machine learning algorithms learns from the data and builds models. Model is a system that finds and predicts based on the input parameters given that are used to make decisions and learn from the system. It observes the data and identifies the differences and facilitates its learning. The algorithm trains the model by searching for patterns in the data and then comes up with the result.

Artificial Intelligence (AI), Machine Learning (ML) being used interchangeably in today's computer programming world. These terms overlap and can be easily confused if one doesnt dive deeper into it. Machine learning is the subset of AI, which means all machine learning is counted as AI, but not every AI is machine learning. For example, symbolic logic, expert systems, and knowledge graphs are AI but they are not machine learning. The machine learning algorithms include decision tree, clustering, inductive logic programming, reinforcement learning, etc. The aspect that separates these from being machine learning is they are not dynamic and will not modify itself when exposed to more data. If AI is mimicking human behavior, then Machine Learning is mimicking human learning.

Machine learning is a form of Artificial Intelligence in which algorithms process and interpret data to recognize patterns by comparing the data with preset rules or inputs. The technology depends on earlier data that it uses to identify any new data to classify it or to execute a predetermined output. Thus, it depends on stored instructions in the form of structured or labeled data. In other words, machine learning requires a programmer to define objects or data for it to recognize them and execute the required action. The initial data and commands provide the technology with the ability to compare any new data with it. The initial input of data for future comparison is called training. Machine learning thus requires training for it to recognize similar data in the future to determine what preprogrammed command to execute. The system becomes better with further exposure to data for training and hence improves in its capacity to recognize similar data in the future. The need to define or label data in advance makes machine learning a supervised form of artificial intelligence [25]. There are three main types of machine learning: supervised, unsupervised, and semi-supervised machine learning. A supervised algorithm learns from labeled data and learns how to classify or perform regression on similar data. For this particular algorithm, a specifically labeled training data set is allotted which is manually allotted. As the algorithm learns from the data, its classification of similar data sets starts to gain more accuracy. On the other hand, an unsupervised machine learning algorithm looks at any given unlabeled data set to find patterns such as clusters. The semi-supervised algorithm is a hybrid of both a supervised and unsupervised algorithm.

2. The Benefits of AI and Machine Learning in Education

Machine Learning, AI, and Data Analytics have been used to maximize students' learning and success. They have been widely applied to track student performances and extract key insights into how these could be improved. These technologies help institutions gain a holistic perspective about their students. Machine Learning and Data Analytics can help teachers identify the learning behaviors of their students, which can lead to improved understanding and better grades for these students. They also allow institutions to accommodate their students' interests and make informed choices that allow them to excel in campus activities.

Before diving into the specific real-world applications of AI and Machine Learning in education and the methodology of their implementation, it is worth taking a moment to summarize what makes these new technologies attractive to educators and students. In a nutshell, AI and Machine Learning could provide substantial benefits to both students and educators in the following areas:

Personalized Learning

AI and Machine Learning, along with data analytics, have the potential to create personalized learning experiences to deal with different challenges. In the past, teachers have noted that "not every student needs the same homework exercise," but it would be absurd to ask a human instructor to tailor each assignment to the various needs of their different students [2]. Some students might find a particular subject easy while the others might have some doubts or difficulty in that subject. This is why the assignment or homework needs to be personalized for each student but it is difficult to do so each time. However, this level of personalization could easily become possible with AI. This approach if brought to implementation will allow each student to enjoy a curriculum and content uniquely tailored to their needs and could improve the motivation and engagement of students in studies. Additionally, such an approach could help teachers to understand the learning styles of each student and help them accordingly.

Smarter Grading

AI and Machine Learning can help in grading work. They have the potential and capability to help in grading work.

Career Suggestions for High School Students

Another promising application for AI & Machine Learning in the education sector could be providing career suggestions for high school students [7]. Intelligent AI-based recommendation systems could collect information of different parameters related to the students' like their academic records, the standardized scores on tests, career dreams, etc. and offer recommendations based on this data.

Student Engagement in Studies

AI tools that monitor student engagement in studies could be extremely useful. Machine Learning, AI, and data analytics could play an important role in keeping students engaged in studies. At the simplest level, they could be leveraged to detect when a student in a remote session is not attentive and nudge them to remind them to pay attention to what is being taught. At the most complex, researchers are testing AI-based frameworks that can successfully detect boredom and engagement in studies using keystrokes, which would allow online teachers to redirect the student's attention accordingly just like an in-person instructor might do [8].

These are just a few of the potential possibilities and uses of AI technologies in the field of education. By offering more personalized, flexible, inclusive, and engaging learning experiences, these technologies have the potential to make virtual classrooms more meaningful and productive. And the future they represent is not far off; in fact, many such applications for AI are already being tested or put to implementation at initial small scale.

3. Real World Applications of AI and ML in Education

Educational Data Mining

One key area of application for AI and ML is Educational Data Mining (EDM). EDM is the practice of collecting student data and apply data mining to personalize education and generate new insights about learning. The data mining methods include classification, clustering, association analysis, and outlier analysis. The classification is a process of finding a set of models for the sake of predictions. Clustering analyzes data objects and creates meaningful groups called clusters. For example, clustering can be used to identify groups students based on their learning styles or class performances or any other metric so that individualized or small group targeted learning can be applied. The main goal of data mining is to reveal previously unknown, implicit, non-trivial patterns and potentially useful knowledge from data.

EDM methods have been used in the past to determine the effectiveness of various pedagogical approaches by measuring student learning in real-time. Researchers have also been able to use EDM to determine whether a particular student is off-task, bored, or frustrated [9,10]. Such methods have obvious advantages for online learning, as teachers can't monitor the attention and engagement of their students as easily in such environments. But with the help of AI systems that collect and analyze large amounts of student data, teachers could be made aware of when their students' attention was beginning to wane. This kind of real-time data could be a helpful substitute for some of the essential non-verbal cues that teachers have lost access to in the shift away from face-to-face instruction.

Student models created through EDM could also lead to more personalized e-learning. Even a university with over 100,000 students could use these student models—updated continuously via AI technologies—to create customized programs for each individual learner. Every student learns in different ways, and the topics they excel at are also different. Instead of having a universal curriculum for all students to follow, customizing the content of every student's classes could optimize teaching to help students only where required. This will benefit the students by making sure they learn as per the requirement and without wasting time on already understood subjects. Of course, this is only one dimension that courses can be customized with, and a wide assortment of adjustments can be made by AI algorithms to personalize the contents of a class for each student.

Intelligent Tutoring Systems (ITS)

Intelligent Tutoring Systems (ITS) use AI to simulate one-on-one human tutoring by providing both extensive knowledge of their subjects and the ability to respond to instantaneous changes in students' behavior and motivation. Intelligent Tutoring Systems could be helpful for teachers and students. Learners at times do not try to completely absorb the knowledge being given by human tutors or miss out certain curriculum concepts so in such cases the Intelligent Tutoring Systems could help. Primarily, ITSs are viewed as AI technology that work best to supplement and help teachers and not replace them [1].

Thanks to AI and Machine Learning, it is possible to identify the unique needs of each student and take or propose relevant action in real-time to address these needs without disrupting the education process. If mode of learning becomes more digital, they could become essential parts of the online classrooms of the future.

AI Chatbots

AI chatbot can be adopted in the field of education. Chatbots are typically used to interact with students and answer common questions. Students can get answers to their common questions from chatbots at any time.

One additional benefit of having chatbots available 24/7 for all kinds of questions is the vast amount of data that would be collected about the concerns and interests of students. This data could be used as input for further data analytics and Machine Learning to extract insightful and actionable knowledge that could help to develop solutions to students' problems and innovative new services to address the interests of students at large.

The University of Murcia in Spain is among the universities to use AI chatbots to interact with students and answer their questions. In just its first year of piloting, the chatbots were able to answer close to 40,000 questions, with an impressive 91% accuracy [19]. In addition to this success, officials also reported that the chatbot increased student motivation and interest.

Staffordshire University in the UK also rolled out chatbots to answer students' questions 24/7. They found one side benefit of such AI-based chatbots is that they allow professors more time to focus on instruction, high-quality teaching material development, and research [19].

Personalized Learning Systems

AI is also transforming students' learning through its implementation in Personalized Learning Systems (PLS). A PLS aims to deliver personalized learning unique to student needs that are identified by analyzing data generated during student interaction with learning resources. Such an AI-enabled PLS can not only process vast amounts of data but it can also scale up easily. A PLS could potentially scale to applications with tens of millions of students, identifying issues from data and generating customized recommendations for each student that is specific to their needs.

4. Using AI & Machine Learning for Efficient School Operations and Automation

Managing and proper allocation of resources is the crucial factor in the education system, where data is the key to efficiency. For example, effective use of data mining on school data can provide insight into the enrollment numbers of different class sections.

Automation is one the simplest application of AI and often provides the most immediate benefit. By automating tasks such as grading, digital asset categorization or timetable scheduling, educator's time will be saved and they utilize this time in other work like interacting with students for clearing their doubts in concepts of curriculum, etc. Entrusting a set of routine tasks to AI can help teachers make room for something more important [29]. Another example of using AI and ML for efficient school operations is to automate data collection and apply data analysis to identify emerging trends especially in higher education. By identifying trends, schools can develop relevant new classes that will be useful for students, like by tracking popular industry certifications courses, education classes and programs for such certifications can be started and teaching strategies can be customized as per the requirement.

Challenges

AI and Machine Learning applications in education are expanding rapidly but this rapid expansion of the technology does not come without challenges and concerns.

Data Privacy, Security, and Ethics

In order to benefit fully from AI, Machine Learning, and Data Analytics, data must be readily available, and many proponents of AI technology simply assume that it will be. In order to make decisions about learning and give feedback customized and tailored to the individual needs of each student, the students' curriculum data would need to be made available to programmers, data analysts, and data scientists but this raises important questions about privacy and data ownership. Hence, utmost care would be required to be taken to ensure data privacy and security is maintained and data ownership issues do not arises and the data ownership remains with the respective students whom the data belongs to. It is important that AI companies use data transparently and ethically. Student curriculum data privacy and protection measures need to be considered and implemented in any data warehousing and data lake solutions that enable data analytics.

Need for Initial Time and Effort Investment

One major goal of Machine Learning is to automate simple tasks that would require a large time investment from educators. These technologies promise to allow instructors more time to focus on valuable person-to-person teaching or doubt clearing of curriculum concepts but there is some concern that these using these technologies based systems would require some sort of training and methods to be learnt in order to handle things efficiently in cases of some technical errors or issues. Asking teachers to acquire the training of efficiently handling and utilizing different technologies based systems like big data and analytics based systems, AI-ML based systems, etc. may initially during the training period cut into the very time that the AI-technologies were intended to save. All of this could mean the need for higher initial costs, and high initial investments by educators to learn and adapt to these new applications. This has been one major point of concern.

Loss of Soft Skills

Many of the above uses of AI are attempts to replicate the benefits of in-class learning in an online environment. In times like the present, when in-class learning is no longer an option due to precautions regarding pandemic, this becomes an essential function for AI. But this doesn't mean that AI can or should fully replace in-person learning. Much of what is learned in a classroom is not the course content itself but the attendant "soft skills" that students gain from the social experience of the classroom. These soft skills are an essential part of learning, and no matter how sophisticated our gadgets become, all of us still have a fundamental need to be part of meaningful classroom communities. The classroom community is what makes learning fun, and it creates a peer-to-peer accountability mechanism that encourages skills such as time-management and group cooperation. The future of AI-based educational technologies will need to be aware of this need and strike a balance between the value of personalized teaching and the need for cohesion and classroom community.

Lack of Human Interaction & Role Models

There is plenty of evidence to suggest that students learn well with genuine teacher interactions. For that reason, the idea of introducing automation into education has raised some concerns. And indeed, the rapid shift to online instruction has made the importance of real student-teacher interaction even more clear. But AI doesn't have to be a threat to student-teacher interactions or try to mimic and replace them. Yes, AI can be great for creating personalized learning customized for each student and providing immediate feedback, but it will be important to find the right balance of AI use in the classroom. Teachers will always play a crucial role in our society, as one must never underestimate the value of human interaction and critical thinking in the field of education [24]. As the applications of these technologies in the field of education increases and even becomes the norm, the optimum results will still be the product of a balanced combination of human strengths and AI capabilities. Although it is clear that AI and Machine Learning algorithms can help to guide decisions significantly, there will always be a need for human interaction, especially for younger students. Educators, school administrators, and policymakers should never lose sight of the importance of the human element that is critical for human development, soft skills, and much more and not allow educational activities to be performed solely by robots and algorithms.

5. Education in a Post-Pandemic World

In 2020, the COVID-19 pandemic transformed the way the K-12 and higher education is carried out. Schools and colleges were shut down for months, and the ones that opened after many months at different places where the pandemic condition improved, saw a reduced number of students, with many parents opting to continue their children's education in online mode only instead of sending them to school. Most teachers are still working remotely, and parents—who are often working remotely themselves—are being asked to help their kids with schoolwork more than ever. Some online education or hybrid online and face-to-face programs already existed, but they had not been implemented at a very large scale unlike in pandemic times where entire curriculum is being taught online using Learning Managing Systems (LMS) and video conferencing options but even existing LMS platforms could continue to improve through the use of artificial intelligence that merges content with evaluation and allows educators to efficiently monitor and track the students' progress. There have been significant developments and breakthroughs in the world of AI and Machine Learning over the last couple of decades, and these technologies give educators the ability to extract key insights about individual students, identify bottlenecks, diagnose issues that prevent student learning, and develop customized learning materials using the vast amount of data being collected through their LMS. Now that the pandemic has made such learning platforms a necessity rather than a luxury, the possibilities for data analysis and algorithmic innovation is unlimited. A well-configured LMS enriched with AI and Machine Learning capabilities will enhance personalize learning, provide immediate feedback, and customize the online learning experience especially in the world of post-pandemic education.

6. The future of AI & Machine Learning in Education

As discussed so far, AI & Machine Learning has very impressive and promising applications in education but as AI technology is continuing to advance, its future applications could surpass even the most optimistic possibilities stated in this chapter. However, there are different challenges with applications of AI and ML in education sector as well which were also discussed in the chapter. The challenges need to be dealt with and optimum solutions should be brought out. In the next section, a few promising applications of AI & ML and other technologies that have direct implications to using AI& ML in education are highlighted.

Internet of Things (IoT) in Education

The Internet of Things have great potential to be used in education. When IoT coupled with Machine Learning and AI, IoT can be very helpful in education.

Virtual Reality (VR), Augmented Reality (AR) Technologies in Education

VR and AR devices have been widely used in mostly gaming and entertainment sectors but these technologies have potential and scope to be used in education sector as well. If these technologies are used along with AI and Machine Learning in education sector, it could turn out to be very useful for the education sector.

7. Conclusion

Artificial Intelligence (AI) and Machine Learning technologies are poised to transform the traditional education. With the technological advancements, COVID-19 pandemic, the need and preference of online/remote education, ever changing tide of how to carry on during pandemic, AI-powered tools have become critical for teachers and students than ever before. AI-powered systems provide students the best opportunities to showcase their abilities by maximizing the limits of their strengths and weaknesses and motivating them to continue their pursuit of knowledge and education. On the other side of the spectrum, teachers are benefitting by being provided with a highly intelligent tool that analyzes and helps them learn about their students curriculum related strengths and weakness and the most effective methods for teaching them specifically to combat with the obstacles of online teaching in the classrooms of today. It is difficult for the teachers to specifically personalize learning for each student as per the requirement and understand all the habits and learning pattern of all the students in the classroom. An AI system powered with latest machine Learning algorithms can help in personalizing learning and analyzing the learning patterns of the students and give suggestions accordingly. AI can analyze and compile the multiple aspects of a student's strengths, weaknesses and learning habits, and can personalize and present the curriculum concepts to students.

Automating grading though AI, can be really helpful for the teachers and can save their time. AI-based recommendation systems can also be utilized to help provide customized career suggestions for students based on test scores, academic records, and overall career aspirations.

In this chapter major AI & Machine Leaning applications in education were presented.

AI stands poised to be a transformational force in education. Like any other technology, the design, implementation should carefully be planned, and the human teaching students pattern should be continued and AI and ML should be included only to help the students and teachers. With non-stopping nature of advancement in AI and Machine Learning, the possibilities are endless, and it will take time to implement these technologies into education ecosystem delicately, efficiently and successfully. All the factors need to be carefully assessed before implementing these technologies so that solutions for issues that are present or can arise in the education world can be found using AI tools to help create a better education system for all.

References

[1] Southgate, E., Blackmore, K., Pieschl, S., Grimes, S., McGuire, J., & Smithers, K. (2019) Artificial Intelligence and Emerging Technologies in Schools, A Research report Commissioned by the Australian Government Department of Education

[2] Hutson, Matthew (2021). Who needs a teacher? Artificial intelligence designs lesson plans for itself. Science Magazine.

[3] Wang, H. C., Chang, C. Y., & Li, T. Y. (2008) Assessing creative problem-solving with automated text grading. Computers & Education, 51(4), 1450–1466.

[4] Abbott, R. G. (2006) Automated expert modeling for automated student evaluation. International Conference on Intelligent Tutoring Systems Springer, Berlin, Heidelberg, pp. 1–10.

[5] Kucak, D., Juricic, V. and Dambic, G. (2018) Machine Learning in Education—A Survey of Current Research Trends. Proceedings of the 29th DAAAM International Symposium, B. Katalinic (Ed.), DAAAM International, Vienna, Austria, pp.0406–0410.

[6] Alice Liu, Back to the Future Classroom: VR/AR/AI Transformation, https://www.eqoptech.org/publications/2020/8/22/back-to-the-future-classroom-vrarai-transformation

[7] Gorad, N., Zalte, I., Nandi, A., & Nayak, D. (2017) Career counselling using data mining. International Journal of Innovative Research in Computer and Communication Engineering.

[8] Bixler, R. and D'Mello, S.K. (2013) Detecting boredom and engagement during writing with keystroke analysis, task appraisals, and stable traits. Proceedings of the 2013 International Conference on Intelligent User Interfaces, p. 225.

[9] D'Mello, S.K., Craig, S.D., Witherspoon, A.W., McDaniel, B.T. and Graesser, A.C. (2008) Automatic detection of learner's affect from conversational cues. User Modeling and User-Adapted Interaction, 18, 45–80.

[10] Baker, R.S.J.D. (2007) Modeling and Understanding Students' Off-Task Behavior in Intelligent Tutoring Systems. Proceedings of the ACM CHI 2007: Computer-Human Interaction Conference, 1059-1068

[11] Dekker, G., Pechenizkiy, M. and Vleeshouwers, J. (2009) Predicting Students Drop Out: A Case Study. Proceedings of the International Conference on Educational Data Mining, Barnes, T., Desmarais, M., Romero, C., and Ventura, S. (eds.), Cordoba, Spain, 41-50.

[12] Romero, C., Ventura, S., Espejo, P.G. and Hervas, C. (2008) Data Mining Algorithms to Classify Students. Proceedings of the 1st International Conference on Educational Data Mining, 8-17.

[13] Superby, J.F., Vandamme, J.P. and Meskens, N. (2006) Determination of factors influencing the achievement of the first-year university students using data mining methods. Proceedings of the Workshop on Educational Data Mining at the 8th International Conference on Intelligent Tutoring Systems, 37-44.

[14] Arnold, Kimberly & Pistilli, Matthew (2012) Course signals at Purdue: Using learning analytics to increase student success. ACM International Conference Proceeding Series. 10.1145/2330601.2330666.

[16] Graesser, A. C., Li, H., & Forsyth, C. (2014). Learning by communicating in natural language with conversational agents. Current Directions in Psychological Science, 23(5), 374-380. doi:10.1177/0963721414540680

[17] Kulik, J.A. and Fletcher, J.D. (2016) Effectiveness of intelligent tutoring systems: a meta-analytic review. Review of Educational Research, 86(1), 42-78.

[18] US Department of Education (2011) Winning the education future: the role of ARPA-ED.

[19] McNeal, Marguerite (2016) A Siri for Higher Ed Aims to Boost Student Engagement. EdSurge-Digital Learner in Higher ED.

[20] Hao, Karen (2019) China has started a grand experiment in AI education. It could reshape how the world learns. MIT Technology Review.

[21] Settles, Burr & Meeder, Brendan. (2016). A Trainable Spaced Repetition Model for Language Learning. 1848-1858. 10.18653/v1/P16-1174.

[22] Bisen, I., Arslan, E., Yildirim, K., Yildirim, Y., "Artificial Intelligence and Machine Learning in Higher Education," Machine Learning Approaches for Improvising Modern Learning Systems edited by Gulzar, IGI Global, May, 2021.

[23] Klein, Alyson (2019) Can artificial intelligence predict student engagement? Researchers investigate. Education Week.

[24] Rouhiainen, Lasse (2019) How AI and data could personalize higher education. Harvard Business Review.

[25] Kersting K. (2018). Machine learning and Artificial Intelligence: Two fellow travelers on the quest for intelligent behavior in machines. Frontiers in Big Data, 1(6). doi: 10.3389/fdata.2018.00006

[26] Radu, Iulian. (2014). Augmented reality in education: A meta-review and cross-media analysis. Personal and Ubiquitous Computing. 18. 1533-1543. 10.1007/s00779-013-0747-y.

[27] Fletcher, J. D. (2011) DARPA Education Dominance Program: April 2010 and November 2010 Digital Tutor Assessments. 31.

[28] Guo, J., Bai, L., Yu, Z., Zhao, Z., & Wan, B. (2021). An AI-Application-Oriented In-Class Teaching Evaluation Model by Using Statistical Modeling and Ensemble Learning. Sensors (Basel, Switzerland), 21(1), 241.

[29] Doug Bonderud (2019), Artificial Intelligence, Authentic Impact: How Educational AI is Making the Grade. Ed Tech Magazine.

London International Conferences

londonic.uk

ukeyconsultingpublishing.co.uk

Keep the libraries running! The crucial role of the volunteers

Christina Schabasser
University of Applied Sciences Burgenland
christina.schabasser@live.at

Abstract

Keeping life stresses away would improve the quality of life, especially in challenging times like the current Covid-19 pandemic. The role of reading in dealing with critical phases of people's lives is remarkable. Public libraries as local information centers encourage reading habits in children and remove gaps between those who are well-informed and those who do not. To continue to fulfill the educational mandate and keep libraries running, addressing the issue of volunteering is necessary. Without the voluntary commitment of the public, a substantial number of libraries may not be able to survive. Focusing on the Austrian library landscape, this study provides recommendations on volunteerism in libraries which are based on interviews and literature analyses.

Keywords: libraries, volunteering, voluntary work in libraries

1. Introduction

The immediate effects of reading on reducing stress are
surprising. According to a study conducted towards 22 stress-
plagued students, a 30-minute reading session lowers blood
pressure, heart rate and feelings of psychological distress
(Rizzolo et al., 2009). A study even found out that people who
read live longer than those who do not. It was observed that
readers have a lower risk of mortality up to 20 percent (Bavishi
et al., 2016). This shows that the healthy and life-enhancing
effects of reading should not be understated.

Public libraries stimulate people's enjoyment of reading and
foster reading competence even among young children. They
offer access to information to all people regardless of their
economic situation. This helps prevent the gap between those
who are well-informed and those who do not by serving as a
tool for promoting the equality of opportunities (Gill et al.,
2004).

Nowadays, public libraries face many challenges caused by
technological advancements. Some of these challenges include
digitization, flood of information, budget cuts, staff reductions
and changes in users' habits and demand (Schuring, 2017).

The future of public libraries seems to be inextricably
tied to the voluntary work because most of the employees in
libraries are indeed volunteers. Therefore, it is safe to say that
volunteers are likely to be indispensable for the library system.
In fact, Austria's public library system is strongly influenced
by voluntary work (Büchereiverband Österreichs, 2021).

This study involved interviews that were carried out at libraries
in Lower Austria, which showed that librarians do recognize
the benefits that volunteers bring to libraries. For example,
there are more programs that can be offered with the help of
volunteers. However, the study also reported that there were
areas of tension between librarians and volunteers existing.

The interviews investigated the work of volunteers at libraries from different perspectives. The outcomes of the interviews provide the basis for the development of several recommendations. For instance, since the interviews concluded that the majority of library workers are female, a recommendation on how libraries could recruit men as volunteers is proposed.

The first section of this paper presents the landscape of the Austrian library system. The second section, meanwhile, outlines the outcomes of the interviews and the third section discusses the findings and presents the recommendations that could be considered by public libraries in Austria.

2. Austria´s public library landscape

According to the statistics by Büchereiverband Österreichs, there are 1.185 public libraries in Austria, excluding special libraries and 43 branchless public libraries that do not provide up-to-date data. Whereas a proper library law that ensures the existence of public libraries does exist in 27 other EU countries, there is no such law existing in Austria. This is another reason for this study to dedicate more time and effort to the subject of volunteer work in public libraries. In Austria, the establishment and operation of public libraries are purely based on voluntary services supported by their providers, like municipalities, towns, and parishes. That is one of the reasons why public libraries in Austria are very different in terms of space, equipment, and staffing (bvoe.at; Leitner et al., 2009).

It was discovered that 189 of the 1185 public libraries in Austria are operated full-time in which at least one librarian is employed as a part-time staff, while 187 public libraries have at least one staff of the institution that supports them who is responsible for the operation of the library as part of his or her employment. This particular staff most likely comes from the municipality. Meanwhile, 809 public libraries are operated by pure volunteers. (see Figure 1).

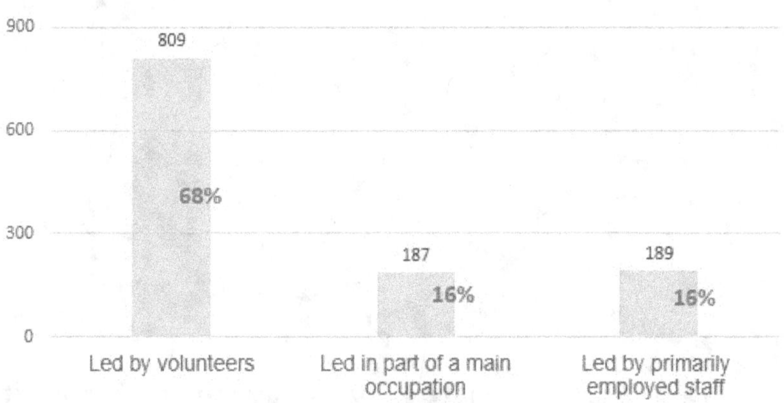

Figure 1. The high share of volunteer-led libraries in Austria

Source: own representation, underlying data from bvoe.at

A glance at the share of library users within Austria's population in 2020 showed that 21,8% of them were children aged between 0 and 13 years old, while 15,4% were teenagers and 5,8% were adults (see figure 2). This indicates that younger children are the main users of public libraries in Austria.

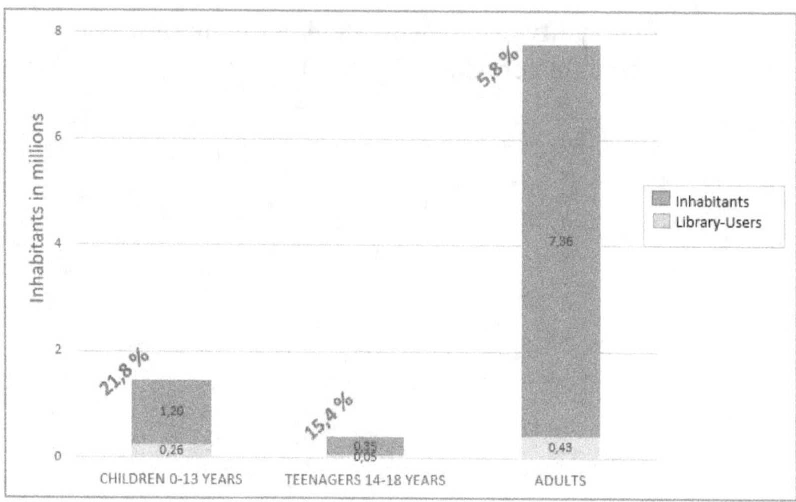

Figure 2. Share of library users in population in 2020

Source: own representation, underlying data from bvoe.at

3. Insights from interviews

Semi-structured interviews were conducted with librarians in Lower Austria. The researcher analyzed the transcribed text precisely to identify any major theme and sub-themes that emerged from the data. The following section, meanwhile, presents the typical works carried out by volunteers at the public libraries in Australia.

3.1. Scope of work of volunteers

- Homepage maintenance (keeping the content up-to-date)

- Support with the children's afternoons

- Support with all work for which the librarians do not have time

- Graphical work (creating the logo, the posters, visiting cards)

- Book-inventory management

- Online library services registrations, de-registrations, and revisions

- Media purchase

3.2. Librarian's opinion on hiring volunteers

Throughout the interviews, the researcher came across a number of interesting and thought-provoking responses. When asked about her opinion on the idea that a library hires volunteers in addition to "normal" employees, for instance, a female head librarian of a public library that is open 7 hours a week and is operated by 15 volunteers and 1 man answered *"I found it hard to imagine, because there are those who get paid and those who don't. But I think this could be a good opportunity for newcomers or people who are looking for additional employment because they don't have to do everything; They can just do what they enjoy."*

Another female volunteer manager of a library that is operated by 13 volunteers commented *"Well, my team that is falling apart at the moment because as a volunteer I cannot oblige them to do anything. They are members of the library, they read for free and they spend a lot of time doing it. Many volunteers think that if they do a service twice or three times a year and help out at an event, then that's more than enough. If people were employed then they would have an obligation. Over the years I have come to know that it is difficult to work with so many volunteers because everyone comes and goes and does and does not do, and a little chaos develops."*

3.3. Pros and cons of employing volunteers

Pros

- It offers more library programs

- It promises new inputs, more diversified ideas, and fruitful exchange

- It changes the team spirit

- It offers flexibility in content with no rigid plan in the background)

- It creates more flexible fields of application also in terms of time

Cons

- The volunteers are not additional, they take the hours from the employees

- There is no obligation for volunteers. A female head of library with 13 volunteers in total said "I have two female seniors as volunteers and they are currently contesting a little on who does more and who is more active and who does it better. One always looks for mistakes in the other. But as I said, they're volunteers, I'm glad I have them."

- It takes extra effort to guide and lead the volunteers. A female manager of a library that was operated by three employees and four volunteers said "Even a volunteer must be led and directed in the same way as someone who is employed, and he must be just as reliable as someone who is employed. That means, I must be able to rely on the two ladies who bind the books, that they will be there on Wednesday morning, so that the books can be delivered on Monday."

- It weakens the values of competency and professionalism since if anyone can do the job anyway, then there is no need for professional and full-time employees. A female library manager brought up the following example "if someone says, well, the volunteers can also hand out books, then I answer why, then all mothers can become teachers because they also have to do homework with the child in the afternoon."

3.4. Possible motives for volunteering

- Personal satisfaction

- Love for the book

- Social life

- Form of contribution to society

- Skill-honing opportunity

- Sense of belonging to a community

- Learning experience

- Social interactions

3.5. Expectations of the volunteers

- Reliable

- Fluent in German. A female library manager described *"I don't need a refugee who can't speak German properly. It's like when you have a bread seller who is allergic to bread. He should know a little about books, too."* However, the following statement by a female library manager said *"I have no problems with that. I had a volunteer with me from Romania who unfortunately moved away, otherwise she would still be there. She had a little difficulty with the German language, but if she knows the program, I have no problem."*

- Strong sense of responsibility

- Passionate about books

- Computer literate

- Enjoying contact with customers and children

- Team-oriented

- Regular attendance (also take part in team meetings)

- Must have time. Some interviewees found it important for the volunteers to allocate at least 3 hours a week to work in the library. A female library manager said "It would be important to have three hours a week. Otherwise, the time is too short to even start anything." Another interviewee whose library is open 7 hours a week claimed that her volunteers invest an average of 2 hours a month for the voluntary work in the library. Another female head of a library, however, was more relaxed on this matter. She said "I don't think there is any norm. As far as I understand it, the younger generation or those who have just committed to voluntary work are no longer committed to the long term anyway."

3.6. Expectations

From the interviews, it could be concluded that there is one common expectation shared by interviewees, which is to have more male volunteers. A female library manager whose library has three employees and four volunteers said *"I would like to have a man in the team as a volunteer. But men don't work unpaid, I can tell you right now. Men only work paid, otherwise they don't work."*

In reply to the question "if you take a man as a volunteer, what could be different then?", she answered *"Well, if only women work together, the masculine note is missing. Just like when there are lots of men in the office, the feminine touch is missing. So, we could use a masculine note. Because of course men think differently than women."*

4. Recommendations

The interviews showed that the role of volunteers in libraries is recognized and valued. There is also the awareness that there would be no rosy future for libraries in Austria without volunteers. There were, however, several uncovered areas that could be critically examined, leaving rooms for improvement.

Based on the outcomes of the interviews, the following recommendations were developed:

4.1. Increasing the share of male volunteers in libraries

First of all, it should be mentioned that the work in public libraries is not gender-related. To successfully recruit male volunteers, it may be necessary to determine specific, short-term tasks, projects, or events that they should handle and offer

positions that they find attractive. Options worth considering
are in technology or business (Driggers et al., 2002). Managers
should be aware that there are also short-term volunteers that
tend to be recruited through participation in a specific event,
such as a weekend library program. Such temporary episodic
volunteers provide a few hours or not more than a day of their
time on a one-off basis. Someone who may only work on a
project-basis arrangement is most likely the same as an interim
volunteer who is involved regularly but for a limited time
period. (Rochester, 2006).

4.2. Matching the interests of a volunteer with the job requirements

The interviews show that most librarians are okay with having
certain volunteers wanting to do certain jobs only. They
consider the preferences and passions of the volunteers. But it
was also mentioned that there are volunteers who only want to
give little contribution. This perhaps has something to do with
the fact that the activities are not tailored well enough to their
interests. Therefore, it is important to understand the different
types of volunteers. Is she or he a volunteer with the ability to
learn? Is she or he a ready-made colleague? Is she or he a
person that never rings in with excuses and never forgets
things? Or is it about someone who likes to talk and who wants
to be in constant contact with people? All these questions may
help managers identify the right volunteers to recruit (Harvey,
2013).

4.3. Understanding the time commitment

The interviews showed that it is important for the librarians to
make sure that the volunteers are regularly present so that they
can take part in meetings from time to time and that the whole
thing is worthwhile for the library. The tendency seems to be
that they would rather have fewer volunteers who spend more
time on this matter. To prevent misunderstanding, it is
essential to understand the time commitment a volunteer can
make. One-day clean-up or beautification activities require

little time and effort. Continuous and recurring activities should be given to people who have the necessary time for them (Grossman et al., 2002).

4.4. Realistically assessing training needs

The interviews showed that library managers would give training to volunteers if they are dissatisfied with their work. This implies that the training effort should not be underestimated. Without any initial or continuous training, the concept of volunteering does not work. Volunteers' prior understanding of program goals and their role in accomplishing those goals affects their work. This may increase their involvement in voluntary works. In addition, regular supervision is critical as it helps ensure that volunteers work effectively. The more time a manager devotes to interacting with volunteers, the better job they will deliver (Grossman et al., 2002). Identification with the work in the library can make them long-term volunteers who are willing to invest a lot of time in their volunteer role (Rochester, 2006).

4.5. Perceiving the variety of tasks

The statement made by one of the library heads who claimed that she could not imagine working with a refugee who speaks almost no German given that the number of tasks in a library is very diverse. There is often a broader variety of jobs than assumed. One example could be that a volunteer is sometimes needed to take care of the plants in the library (Driggers et al., 2002).

4.6. Understanding the volunteer´s costs and benefits

It helps a lot to understand the total costs and benefits that a volunteer may offer to the library. The costs that volunteers may need to consider include the amount of time spent at the library, the amount of income that they may lose, and the amount of social interaction that they may give up. The benefits, meanwhile, may include their probability of gaining social reputation, potential of future employment, personal satisfaction, and new experience in organization (Handy et al, 2000) and appreciation. The "NÖ Bibliotheken Award" shows how good the work can be rewarded, especially in the "Personal Commitment" category which is dedicated to volunteers who are willing to give their special commitment to the work (treffpunkt-bibliothek.at). The librarians, meanwhile, should also try to create incentives to provide some benefits to the volunteers.

4.7. Establishing a clear distribution of work between full-time workers and volunteers

Full-time employees expressed their concern over the risk of having their own hours deducted as the library recruits more volunteers. That being said, there is no need for them to worry that their professional competence will be called into question if the division of work between full-time employees and volunteers is clearly defined. In Germany, for instance, core library tasks such as information transfer, process or change management continues to be carried out by specialists and volunteers are hired for tasks that have nothing to do with primary librarianship (Kulzer, 2015).

5. Discussion

The fact that reading may have positive effects on health implies that the existence of public libraries as places of information is quite fundamental as they encourage people to read. However, without the proper commitment of volunteers, public libraries in Austria would face a sad future. This paper shows how important volunteers are for the Austrian public libraries. After a brief introduction to the Austrian library landscape, important insights from the interviews are presented. Citations from the interviewees are also outlined to provide clarifications on what actually happens in the real-life setting. In addition, some recommendations on how volunteer

work in public libraries could be organized in the future are
also presented.

References

Bavishi, Avni; Slade, Martin; Levy, Becca (2016). A chapter a
        day – Association of book reading with longevity.
        Social Science & Medicine. 164.
        10.1016/j.socscimed.2016.07.014.

Büchereiverband Österreichs (2021), Statistics and
        Performance data. Available at
        https://www.bvoe.at/oeffentliche_bibliotheken/statistik
        und_leistungsdaten

Driggers, Preston F.; Dumas, Eileen. Managing Library
        Volunteers: A Practical Toolkit. Chicago: American
        Library Association, 2002

Gill, Philip; Clubb, Barbara; Glashoff, Ilona; Hassner,
        Kerstin; Hayrapetian, Nerses; Pestell, Robert (2004).
        Die Dienstleistungen der Öffentlichen Bibliothek:
        IFLA/UNESCO Richtlinien für die Weiterentwicklung.
        IFLA Publications Series.
        https://repository.ifla.org/handle/123456789/927

Grossman, Jean Baldwin; Furano, Kathryn (2002). Making the
        Most of Volunteers. Public/Private Ventures (P/PV),
        Report/Whitepaper Text, Available at
        https://ppv.issuelab.org/resource/making-the-most-of-
        volunteers.html

Handy, F., R. Cnaan, J. Brudney, U. Ascoli, L. Meijs and S.
        Ranade (2000) 'Public perception of 'who is a
        volunteer': an examination of the net-cost approach
        from a cross-cultural perspective', Voluntas 11 (1).

Harvey, Philip (2013). The Human Factor: Volunteers in
        Libraries. The Anztla EJournal 11, 128 – 134.
        https://doi.org/10.31046/anztla.vi11.276

Kulzer, Gudrun (2015). Ehrenamt in Bibliotheken – Erfolg
        durch professionelles Management. Forum
        Management. Available at

https://www.bibliotheksforum-bayern.de/fileadmin/archiv/2015-3/PDF-Einzelbeitraege/BFB_0315_09_Kulzer_V04.pdf

Leitner, Gerald; Schipfer, Roswitha (2009). Die Zukunft gestalten Chance Bibliothek. Vier Schritte in ein Bibliotheksland Österreich. Available at https://www.bvoe.at/sites/default/files/attachments/chance_bibliothek.pdf

Rizzolo, Denise; Zipp, Genevieve; Simpkins, Susan; Stiskal, Doreen (2009). Stress Management Strategies For Students: The Immediate Effects Of Yoga, Humor, And Reading On Stress. Journal of College Teaching and Learning. 6,79-88. 10.19030/tlc.v6i8.1117.

Rochester, Colin (2006). Making sense of volunteering A literature review. Volunteering England. Available at https://efc.issuelab.org/resource/making-sense-of-volunteering-a-literature-review.html

Schurig, Tina (2017). Die Zukunftsfähigkeit öffentlicher Bibliotheken: Rollen, Chancen und Grenzen - international und national. Wiesbaden: b.i.t. verlag gmbh.

Treffpunkt Bibliothek. Services des Landes NÖ für Bibliotheken. Online: 10. NÖ Bibliotheken Award 2020. Available at https://www.treffpunkt-bibliothek.at/online-10-noe-bibliotheken-award-2020/

London International Conferences

londonic.uk

ukeyconsultingpublishing.co.uk

Reimagining Education with Artificial Intelligence

Emin Alp Arslan
University of Texas at Austin
eminalparslan@gmail.com

Kamil Yildirim
Harmony Science Academy
kamilyildirim24@gmail.com

Ibrahim Bisen
University of Texas at Austin
ebisen2003@gmail.com

Yetkin Yildirim
Rice University
yetkin@rice.edu

Abstract

Artificial intelligence (AI) technologies have been implemented successfully in many industries, from virtual hospital assistants to algorithm-based warehouse processing. And now that Covid-19 has forced students and teachers to transition to online or hybrid learning, these technologies could offer new and exciting possibilities for education as well. By incorporating AI and machine learning tools into online classrooms, educators can address many of the challenges that have emerged with the

E. Arslan
K. Yildirim
I. Bisen
Y. Yildirim

recent loss of face-to-face instruction, including the struggle for students to self-regulate their learning, the burden of curriculum planning and administrative work for teachers, and the loss of personalized interaction between students and teachers. This chapter will explore some of the AI technologies that have been used in educational contexts and describe applications of AI in other industries that could be adapted to create more personalized, flexible, inclusive, and engaging learning experiences. If the future of education is going to include online learning as a substantial component, then AI could be the key to maintaining high levels of motivation and engagement from students and teachers alike.

Keywords: artificial intelligence, machine learning, higher education, intelligent tutoring system, natural language processing, student engagement, administrative tasks, virtual assistants

E. Arslan
K. Yildirim
I. Bisen
Y. Yildirim

Reimagining Education with Artificial
Intelligence

1. Introduction

It is estimated that the average American looks at a screen two hours every day around the nation, and this number only increased with the Covid lockdowns (Wong et al., 2021). This increase can be attributed to the shift online of many aspects of our lives, from education to business. And with this shift comes increased data collection capabilities, which has opened the way for artificial intelligence (AI) and machine learning technologies to penetrate our everyday lives. Nick Bostrom, a leading artificial intelligence expert from Oxford University, has said in an interview with CNN that "[a] lot of cutting-edge AI has filtered into general applications, often without being called AI because once something becomes useful enough and common enough it is not labeled AI anymore" (CNN 2006). Although many of these applications have integrated AI concepts, the fact often goes unnoticed in day-to-day life. Because AI is an interdisciplinary field it is not easy to give it a description. Philosophy, mathematics, economics, neuroscience, psychology, linguistics, and biology all have their own definitions and perspectives on AI, but in order to define AI in the field of computer science, it is important to first explain the concept of machine learning (Luckin et al., 2016). Machine learning systems are computer systems that can analyze and learn from previous data and make predictions. For the purposes of this paper, AI will be defined as a field of computer science that specializes in creating computer systems that are designed to interact with the world and can mimic and operate as human beings by utilizing machine learning. Because our lives have started transitioning online, there has been increased spending and investment in the technology sector. Unfortunately, very few of these investments go toward education. As shown in Figure 1, artificial intelligence spending in the education sector is low compared to many other industries. However, with more non-profit artificial intelligence research companies like the

E. Arslan
K. Yildirim
I. Bisen
Y. Yildirim

OpenAI and The Future Privacy Forum, spending for artificial intelligence in education (AIEd) may increase substantially.

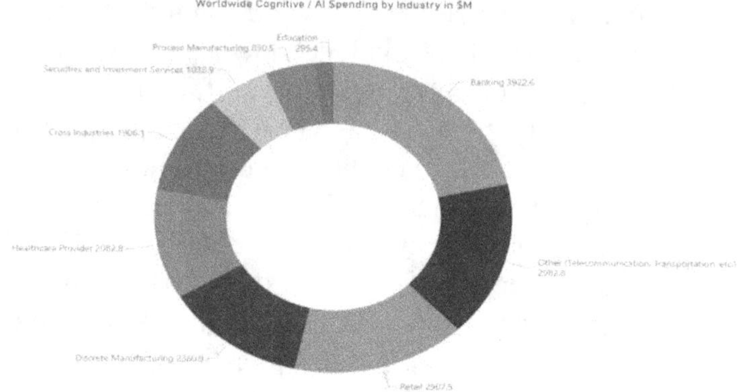

Figure 1. Worldwide Cognitive / AI Spending by industry. From "Artificial Intelligence Spending Quick Look: U.S. Buying Behavior By Industry, Company Size, and LOB Versus IT" by Soohoo, 2020. Own graph.

1.1 Artificial Intelligence and Machine Learning

Before exploring the concepts and the opportunities that AI offers in the education sector, it is important to thoroughly understand the subsections of both artificial intelligence and machine learning. Artificial intelligence can be classified into three subsections: weak, general, and strong AI. Weak artificial intelligence is usually interchangeable with narrow AI because they imply limited capabilities. A weak AI can only perform the tasks that are given to it and cannot overarch to other actions. General artificial intelligence is an AI that can perform any given intellectual task with the performance and efficiency of humans. Strong artificial intelligence is an intelligence system that can surpass any human intelligence and it can perform any human task better than any human. Weak and narrow AI is the most common AI in today's world. Some examples of narrow AI are recommendation algorithms on e-commerce websites, self-driving cars, and speech recognition. Constructing any general or super AI would require a huge operation, a prohibitive budget, and significant human power.

There are three types of algorithms that are most common when creating a machine learning system: supervised, unsupervised, and semi-supervised. A supervised algorithm learns from labeled data and is generally used to classify incoming data. The data set that trains this sort of algorithm needs to be manually labeled for the machine learning algorithm to learn. An unsupervised algorithm can look at any given unlabeled data and perform regressions, perhaps to make future predictions. A semi-supervised algorithm can complete the functions of both supervised and unsupervised algorithms, meaning it uses a small amount of labeled data and a large amount of unlabeled data.

1.2 Benefits of Artificial Intelligence

For students, the transition to an online learning environment brought with it both benefits and drawbacks. It has been especially difficult for educational institutions to transition and meet the needs of their students. Nevertheless, online education delivered a more personalized learning experience for many students with more relaxed deadlines, giving the students the freedom of trial and error without receiving any judgment, and students were able to search and learn the concepts they needed on the spot. By analyzing student data, many schools were able to analyze student progress and even identify knowledge gaps among different groups of students. This transition also enabled companies that were developing artificial intelligence-powered learning platforms to find the marketplace and the consumers that they needed. Online education providers can create and sustain machine learning algorithms that conduct data analysis because it is becoming increasingly easier and cheaper to do so. The improvements that artificial intelligence has provided in our daily lives are immense, and this article only plans to scratch the surface of the benefits that this technological revolution can offer to education through personalized content, automated administrative tasks, and student interaction. These are the areas where artificial intelligence can provide help in education and where current developments are underway (Lynch, 2020).

2. Using Artificial Intelligence to Personalize Education

Perhaps the most important contribution artificial intelligence can make to education is personalization. Using artificial intelligence, student knowledge can be modeled and accounted for when teaching. This makes learning much more efficient and adaptive, as it helps teach students only what they need by recognizing knowledge gaps and understanding their grasp on the subject. Each student's learning preferences are different: some prefer to learn through visuals, some through audio, some through repetition. By customizing the content of every student's curriculum, each student's learning could be optimized to help them in areas where they need it the most. This can eliminate the need for a universal curriculum and students who excel in certain areas can move through these topics faster than their peers. Each student can move at their own pace, making the learning process much more efficient. In these ways, artificial intelligence can fundamentally transform how teaching is done, allowing for a much more adaptable and personalized educational environment. As the Organization for Economic Co-operation and Development (OECD) states, "education needs to start adapting to increasing individualism in societies, and artificial intelligence can help do this" (Lynch, 2020).

2.1 Intelligent Tutoring Systems

One of the primary ways artificial intelligence helps personalize education is through Intelligent Tutoring Systems (ITS). These ITSs help guide students through concepts with

E. Arslan
K. Yildirim
I. Bisen
Y. Yildirim

step-by-step personalized tutorials. The ITS finds the best way to teach the student using its own knowledge on the subject and pedagogy along with its conception of the student's understanding. Then the ITS responds to how the student performs and gives guidance when it finds it appropriate to do so. The ITS must strike a balance between giving away the answer to everything and not giving enough help when it is needed, and these systems typically draw from one of the following models in order to make such decisions: the domain model, the pedagogical model, and the learner model. A typical ITS architecture can be found in Figure 2.

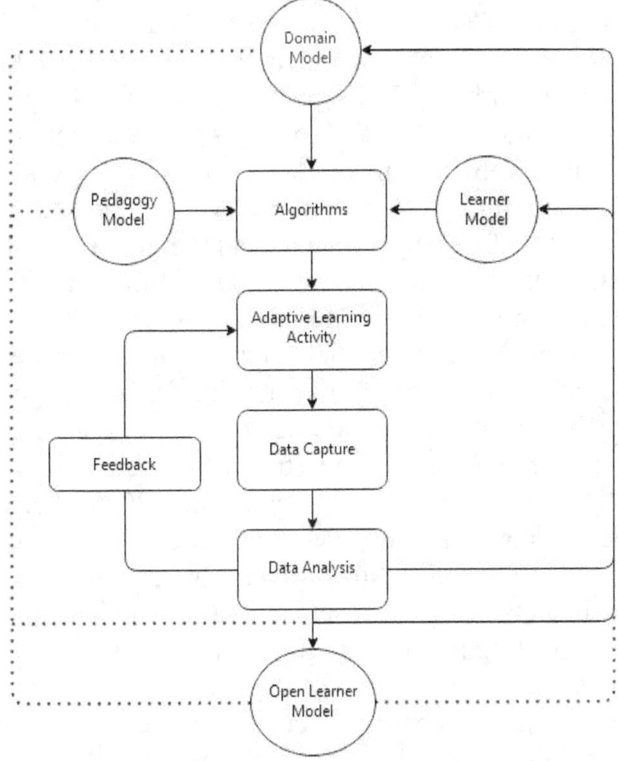

Figure 2. The architecture of a typical Intelligent Tutoring System (ITS) From "Intelligence Unleashed: An Argument for AI in Education" by Luckin et al., 2016. Own diagram.

E. Arslan
K. Yildirim
I. Bisen
Y. Yildirim

The domain model contains the knowledge about the subject being taught. For example, if a mathematics lesson on fractions is being taught, the domain model might include knowledge about the addition and multiplication of fractions. The pedagogical model, on the other hand, represents the most effective approaches to teaching. This model might optimize the best time to help the student with a hint or to review a certain topic. The learner (or student) model considers what the student understands as well as some of their behavioral qualities. This model will track how well a student performs and what concepts the student might not understand along with their emotional state and previous achievements and difficulties (Holmes et al., 2019). There is also an interface component, which is the medium through which the student interacts with the ITS. When used with neural networks (self-training algorithms), these models can constantly improve, learning from each interaction with every student that uses them and finding the best teaching methods to use in specific instances. This way, the ITS can learn to recognize patterns that might have been impossible for humans to find, leading to a much more effective model for teaching.

These models not only help create adaptive learning environments, but they also provide further insight into the mechanics of learning. By personalizing education, educators can learn more about how students learn and the steps they take during this process (Luckin et al., 2016). For example, these adaptive learning systems could help educators find common misconceptions students have while studying mathematics and help them address these discrepancies.

By modeling learners' cognitive and emotional states, an ITS can adapt its feedback type to maximize a positive affective state, which has been proven to increase learning performance (Grawemeyer et al., 2015). In this way the ITS can learn more about what type of feedback might be most effective in specific circumstances, further individualizing the learning experience. ITSs can also use more meta-cognitive frameworks to approach learning, which helps improve student motivation and willingness to learn (Du Boulay et al., 2007). For instance, the use of narrative framing while teaching could be one approach that boosts student motivation (Luckin et al., 2016). Some ITSs might even take the approach of the Socratic method, having the learner engage in dialogue where they repeatedly ask questions to increase their understanding of the subject, leaving the learning more in the hands of the student than the tutor.

ITSs have the possibility to transform learning and increase the opportunity for more individualized teaching. Education can shift towards a more tutor-based approach, where students rely more on their ITS. One-on-one human tutoring is perhaps the most effective teaching method; however, it is impossible for every student to get this treatment in traditional learning contexts. ITS can bridge this gap and help provide feasible and affordable intelligent tutors for every student. An alternative to ITS, called exploratory learning environments (ELE), can help learners by giving them a much more hands-on approach to learning, leaving the students to learn on their own and guiding the students when needed (Holmes et al., 2018). The student is exposed to and experiences the concept rather than simply being told about it. Because of this, ELE tend to be more unstructured and up to the learners, giving up some control in exchange for a more self-sufficient learning experience for the student. This way a much more student-based approach to learning can be achieved.

In practice, ITSs have been very successful at increasing both student performance and motivation. For example, the Andes Physics Tutoring System is an ITS that helps guide students through their physics homework. As the student solves each problem, the ITS gives feedback, significantly improving student learning (VanLehn et al., 2005). If an ITS that solely helps with homework can increase student performance significantly, it is reasonable to think that a more sophisticated ITS at the center of an entire course would be even more effective. ITSs might not only help increase student performance, but also reduce learning time, giving students more time to focus on other activities. Another example of a successful ITS is Carnegie Learning's Cognitive Tutor, a mathematics course with textbook resources and an automated cognitive tutor. This ITS focuses on real-world problem solving with mathematics primarily for students aged 13 to 17. Cognitive Tutor has been shown to improve average student performance by about 50% to 60% (Holmes et al., 2018).

2.2 Educational Data Mining

AIEd has also helped many schools through educational data mining (EDM). By analyzing data about students and their behavior, data analysts can predict their likelihood of dropping out, among other important factors (Luckin et al., 2016). This type of data mining can also help educators gauge their teaching abilities and test out different teaching methods, since they can analyze the effect these different styles of teaching have on the performance of the students. EDM could also help replace tests and exams as the primary way to assess student knowledge by helping educators track student performance while taking many more factors into consideration (Hill et al., 2014). Through EDM, educators can better understand how a student answers a question and why a student gave a particular answer, rather than whether they got the question right or wrong. This way, students can be assessed as they learn, rather than having to interrupt their education for assessments to take place. These learning analytics can also provide further insights into when students need assistance throughout their education, and reveal more about their successes and challenges, along with their motivation throughout their learning process (Luckin et al., 2016). All these things that the use of EDM unlocks can help not only personalize learning but also provide a better and more motivational environment for students to learn in.

E. Arslan
K. Yildirim
I. Bisen
Y. Yildirim

3. Using Artificial Intelligence in Administrative Tasks

The implementation of artificial intelligence in administrative tasks can help educational institutions save great amounts of money. As technology progresses, the implementation of technologies like artificial intelligence becomes cheaper and cheaper. Therefore, it becomes inefficient to pay administrators to do jobs that can be automated by artificial intelligence. Although automation is a concern for many, ultimately, it would have a positive effect for educational institutions, as artificial intelligence can do many of the repetitive administrative tasks required of both teachers and administrators. Because of this, the implementation of artificial intelligence in administrative tasks would ease the workload of teachers and administrators and make it easier for them to focus on what is important. This would also mean that the implementation of artificial intelligence in this area would not be a threat to student-teacher interactions which is an essential aspect of learning. In fact, by easing the workload of teachers and administrators, it could, instead of replacing them, make their roles more student centric.

3.1 Artificial Intelligence for Grading

One of those repetitive administrative tasks, perhaps the most prevalent for teachers, is grading. Grading takes up a great deal of teachers' time. But imagine if teachers did not have to spend hours grading assignments and could instead spend more time interacting with their students. Moreover, grading by artificial intelligence may actually be more reliable in some cases, as teachers are often subject to unintentional biases. (Murphy, 2019) There could be many benefits to using artificial intelligence instead of teachers to grade assignments, and in fact, many artificial intelligence grading tools already exist for teachers to use. Gradescope, for example, is an online grading tool for higher education that uses artificial intelligence (UMass Lowell, n.d.). With tools like these, the possibility for biased grading can be greatly reduced. Artificial intelligence

E. Arslan
K. Yildirim
I. Bisen
Y. Yildirim

could also be used to detect plagiarism and cheating, which would provide more appropriate grading, since these cases can be difficult for teachers to detect. Several workshops at the International Conference on Machine Learning investigated the use of artificial intelligence-powered grading systems that could grade computer assignments at a large scale to decrease the workload of higher education teachers and to reduce the need for teaching assistants (True Interaction, n.d.). Although it is unlikely that artificial intelligence will become a replacement for educators anytime soon, the implementation of artificial intelligence does seem to be a promising way to relieve educators from a variety of their administrative burdens.

The first commercial automated essay scoring systems, Intellimetric and e-rater, were commercially available by the early 1990s (Bisen et al., 2021). Intellimetric has many applications in the industry, and many companies and organizations still use it for tasks like screening job applicants and certification testing. These early scoring systems were utilized by educational institutions too. More recently, organizations like EdX and Coursera that provide extensive open online courses for immense amounts of students have also implemented automated essay scoring systems to their courses to grade student writing. Current automated essay scoring systems can not only give an overall holistic writing quality score for student writing, but they can also give feedback, guidance, and even model writing samples to assist students with improving their writing. Some of these current systems are Turnitin's Revision Assistant, Pearson's Write to Learn, the Copyleaks AI Grader, Grammarly, the Educational Testing Service's Criterion Online Writing Evaluation Service, and Chegg's Writelab. Each of these systems offers a variety of different types of feedback to students (Murphy, 2019). Unfortunately, there have been cases where automated essay scoring systems have produced higher scores than what should have been produced. However, humans are more prone to

E. Arslan
K. Yildirim
I. Bisen
Y. Yildirim

mistakes than automated essay scoring systems, so it is still a viable option even though they still are not efficient enough to replace good writing teachers who spend their time while grading. Nevertheless, as these technologies advance, they could match or even surpass good writing teachers in efficiency.

3.2 Natural Language Processing

Natural language processing, a field of artificial intelligence, is what makes automated essay scoring systems possible. This field analyzes written language by implementing artificial intelligence techniques like machine learning. If natural language processing continues to become more sophisticated, teachers could conceivably be replaced by artificial teachers. Currently, natural language processing plays a huge role in many different industries. For example, it is used in the medical industry to gain insights into medical records and other text data. Because of natural language processing, a team of researchers in Taiwan were able to help determine which stroke patients needed intravenous thrombolysis (Thomas, 2020). Natural language processing is also used in the pharmaceutical industry, where it can help researchers analyze data from all the stages in the drug development process in more efficient and useful ways than before. In addition, natural language processing has been used in the interpretation of clinical trials as well. The financial industry also utilizes natural language processing. Financial institutions have to deal with lengthy legal documents daily, and they can use natural language processing to extract the necessary information from those documents and organize the documents according to certain requirements. Furthermore, natural language processing is used similarly in the insurance industry, in which insurance companies also need to deal with large numbers of lengthy documents.

First developed in the 1950s, natural language processing algorithms are used in text-to-speech applications, language translation applications, and even in virtual speech assistants like Apple's Siri. On the other hand, the algorithms of automated essay scoring systems extract parts of a text and learn the patterns between the parts and different writing levels with natural language processing (Murphy, 2019). Different automated essay scoring systems have different input features based on their goals for providing feedback and scoring (Automated Essay Scoring, 2003). These different input features range from linguistic and nonlinguistic surface features like grammatical errors and the number of words to sentence-level and essay-level qualities like the use of passive voice and style respectively. Additionally, while some automated essay scoring systems provide scores holistically, others give scores and feedback based on individual aspects of the text instead. In most cases, training these automated essay scoring systems can require hundreds or even thousands of essays and many hours of labor by expert graders to analyze and grade essays. However, in the end, the time that these systems can save for teachers greatly exceeds the effort put into making them.

3.3 Scheduling

Scheduling is another repetitive administrative task that must be done every year and that could easily be facilitated by AI technology (Bisen et al., 2021). Creating schedules for students is very tedious and, in many cases, very difficult. Especially in smaller schools, finding a way to give every student their preferred classes can be an impossible task. In bigger schools, even though giving students their preferred classes may be less of a problem, the higher abundance of students also creates challenges. There is simply a larger number of schedules to make and giving students their preferred teachers can be a problem as well. But with artificial intelligence, this process could be greatly streamlined and made more satisfactory for everyone. Artificial intelligence can analyze more possibilities for schedules to make sure that more teachers and students are satisfied with their schedules. Many such implementations of artificial intelligence already exist in the industry. For example, ServiceMax, a Field Service Management company, implements artificial intelligence scheduling software to automate their scheduling processes (ServiceMax, n.d.) Moreover, through the use of algorithms that analyze student behavior and student backgrounds, artificial intelligence could be used to match students and teachers based on the data from those algorithms. This could help improve the bonds between students and teachers by creating points of interest or matching personalities. Also, the implementation of artificial intelligence in scheduling can save school administrators a lot of hassle, giving them more time to help their students.

3.4 Virtual Assistants

Artificial intelligence could also help answer non-course-related questions that would normally be directed to administrators. These questions could be about things such as school events, administration, college application process, and graduation. In addition, artificial intelligence could be used to answer students' course related questions that would normally be directed to teachers. Most large banking companies already implement artificial intelligence in similar ways. For example, HSBC implements an online virtual assistant that is able to answer common queries from customers such as questions about their account details or balance (Thomas, 2020). The implementation of virtual assistants or chatbots like these helps those companies save money by decreasing the need for call centers. Additionally, many companies that have online retail stores have chatbots on their websites too. If educational institutions were to implement virtual assistants or chatbots in similar ways, they too could save money by decreasing the need for large amounts of counselors. They could at least save the counselors' time, allowing them to focus on other important tasks.

E. Arslan
K. Yildirim
I. Bisen
Y. Yildirim

One educational organization, The Common App, recently implemented an artificial intelligence chatbot named Oli to help students throughout the college admissions process. This chatbot was introduced due to the decrease in applications in Fall 2020, a time at which Covid-19 was prevalent. This way, they were able to bring college advising to students' homes at a time where it would have been very difficult to do so. Other educational organizations have implemented chatbots too. Schoolinks, a college and career readiness platform, also implements artificial intelligence in a variety of ways. Its implementation can ease the work for counselors. First of all, they too implement a chatbot to help students with their college applications or career search. Additionally, Schoolinks has career assessments that implement machine learning algorithms (Schoolinks, n.d.). These algorithms help students find careers that fit their personality and courses that fit their interests through the use of artificial intelligence. Schoolinks also uses artificial intelligence to assist students with their college search. By analyzing data about a student's personality obtained through simple tests, Schoolinks can recommend colleges that fit not only the students' merit, but also their personal characteristics. Furthermore, Schoolinks' use of artificial intelligence can benefit students by also providing personalized internship and volunteering opportunities. This platform can benefit school administrators as well by saving them time and bringing them new insights regarding their students.

These virtual assistants could be developed to where they can answer not-so-basic questions that would normally be directed to administrators or even teachers (Bisen et al., 2021). This would allow teachers to focus on their curriculum and teaching and alleviate the stress that comes with having to explain everything about the subject. It would also help make sure all student's questions are answered and teachers/administrators would become the "last resort" for asking questions. This concept would work very well with the previous concept of personalizing education and learning for each student as well. While students work at their own pace, they could ask their questions to a virtual assistant instead of compressing learning into an hour-long class where they have more limited time to think of and ask the questions that they have. On a classroom level, a sufficiently advanced virtual assistant could be a place where students could ask the due date of an assignment, the submission process of a test, details of their next homework, and any other questions about the class itself.

3.5 Tests and Exams

Another important administrative area where artificial intelligence can be of assistance is in the creation of tests and exams (Bisen et al., 2021). This could be as basic as choosing the difficulty of the next question depending on correct question streaks and the performance of the student or perhaps using a question bank to randomly select the questions in a test to prevent students from cheating. AI systems could make testing more effective and decrease the likelihood of cheating. Artificial intelligence could also be used to detect the similarities between students' exams by looking at variables such as time, word usage, submission date, and so on, to identify the students that may be cheating. By enabling teachers to make more effective tests and to identify inappropriate student behavior, the use of artificial intelligence in this area could greatly improve testing and examinations. Pymetrics is a platform that implements artificial intelligence to benefit companies from all types of industries. Pymetrics helps companies with things like choosing the fit candidates for a job and matching members into productive groups. Pymetrics assesses a company's job applicants as well as that same company's top performers. Then it analyzes both of their behavior to find which applicants match. Further, by analyzing current employees, Pymetrics can also help restructure a company in a way that the company would work more efficiently and maximize employee potential. These applications of AI could be useful in a classroom as well. Not only could a platform like Pymetrics be used while hiring teachers and administrators for an educational institution, but the form of artificial intelligence used by Pymetrics could be used to make group-work more productive and organize students with complementary skills into classrooms together.

4. Using Artificial Intelligence in Student Engagement and Interaction

For the last two decades, online education has been gaining popularity. But since its inception in the late 1990s, online education has also raised concerns as to how a remote learning system can keep students attentive and focused (O'Brien, 2002; Tinto, 2006; Truluck, 2007). With the Covid-19 pandemic and lockdowns, many educational institutions had to rely upon online programs to continue teaching their students (Kose et al., 2021). It is already difficult to keep students focused in-person, so how can you expect teachers to keep their students focused in online environments? This is another area where artificial intelligence could prove to be incredibly useful.

When it comes to evaluating student participation, involvement, engagement, and overall success in online education, AI provides teachers with multiple options. Recently the School of Computer Engineering and Science at Shanghai University published a research article talking about how they were able to collect data from a Virtual Learning Environment (VLE), an e-learning system, and used machine learning algorithms to measure student engagement and performance (Hussain et al., 2018). This study analyzed the number of clicks on the webpages of the course such as the forums, the glossary, any subpages, the homepage, and course content and conducted multiple experiments using these algorithms. This experiment was able to find that there was correlation between the students' assessment scores and the students that the study found most engaging according to their clicks (Hussain et al. 2018). Therefore, this study was able to show that artificial intelligence could be used to determine which students are engaged in an online environment. This would give teachers valuable information, as it is often difficult for them to know which of their student are most engaged in an online environment. With the help of this AI, teachers could better reach out to the students in class who need more attention and guidance than their peers.

5. Conclusion

Online education is gaining more and more prominence due to the recent shifts in education brought about by Covid-19. With this in mind, artificial intelligence can play a huge role in this advancement in education. While there are some established uses of artificial intelligence in education today, most applications are experimental, and artificial intelligence uses in other industries are starting to cross over as well. Natural language processing, for example, has been used in many industries for a variety of reasons. Now, natural language processing is being used in the education industry with the introduction of chatbots and automatic essay scoring systems. One of the foremost advantages artificial intelligence can bring to education is personalization with the use of programs like Intelligent Tutoring Systems (ITS). Education data mining (EDM) can also help assess student knowledge in a much more meaningful way. This personalization can bring about a more individualized learning experience for each and every student, increasing both their performance and motivation. AI can also help deal with administrative burdens that teachers and administrators have to go through like grading and scheduling. Finally, artificial intelligence provides an opportunity for increasing the engagement of students, developing self-regulatory skills, and increasing interaction between students, their peers, and their teachers. With all of these benefits in

E. Arslan
K. Yildirim
I. Bisen
Y. Yildirim

mind, the implication of the introduction of artificial intelligence to education is massive and has the possibility to transform the industry.

References

Artificial Intelligence Scheduling Software. ServiceMax. (n.d.). https://www.servicemax.com/field-service-manual/artificial-intelligence-scheduling.

Automated Essay Scoring: A Cross-disciplinary Perspective. (2003). United States: Taylor & Francis.

Becker, S. A., Brown, M., Dahlstrom, E., Davis, A., DePaul, K., Diaz, V., & Pomerantz, J. (2018). Horizon Report 2018 higher education edition brought to you by EDUCAUSE (pp. 1-54). EDUCAUSE.

Bisen, I., Arslan, E., Yildirim, K., Yildirim Y. (2021). Artificial Intelligence and Machine Learning in Higher Education, Machine Learning Approaches for Improvising Modern Learning Systems (Advances in Educational Technologies and Instructional Design), 1-17.

Chen, L., Chen, P., & Lin, Z. (2020). Artificial intelligence in education: a review. IEEE Access, 8, 75264-75278.

CNN. AI set to exceed human brain power. (2006, August 9). Retrieved from http://edition.cnn.com/2006/TECH/science/07/24/ai.bostrom/.

Copyleaks. Ai grading tool - online grade calculator for essays, tests. (n.d.). Retrieved from https://copyleaks.com/education/ai-grading

Deci, E. L., Vallerand, R. J., Pelletier, L. G., & Ryan, R. M. (1991). Motivation and education: The self-determination perspective. Educational psychologist, 26(3-4), 325-346.

Du Boulay, B., Rebolledo-Mendez, G., Luckin, R., Martínez-Mirón, E., & Harris, A. (2007, June). Motivationally

Intelligent Systems: Diagnosis and Feedback. In AIED (pp. 563-565).

Features Gallery. Schoolinks. (n.d.). Retrieved from https://www.schoolinks.com/feature-gallery

Grading Software/Gradescope. UMass Lowell. (n.d.). Retrieved from https://www.uml.edu/IT/Services/Academic-Technology/Grading-Software-Gradescope.aspx

Grawemeyer, B., Mavrikis, M., Holmes, W., & Gutierrez-Santos, S. (2015, June). Adapting feedback types according to students' affective states. In International Conference on artificial intelligence in Education (pp. 586-590). Springer, Cham.

Guilherme, A. (2019). AI and education: the importance of teacher and student relations. Ai & Society, 34(1), 47-54.

Hill, P. W., & Barber, M. (2014). Preparing for a renaissance in assessment. London: Pearson.

Holmes, W., Anastopoulou, S., Schaumburg, H., & Mavrikis, M. (2018). Technology-enhanced personalised learning: Untangling the evidence.

Holmes, W., Bialik, M., & Fadel, C. (2019). Artificial intelligence in education. *Boston: Center for Curriculum Redesign*.

Holstein, K., McLaren, B. M., & Aleven, V. (2018, June). Student learning benefits of a mixed-reality teacher awareness tool in AI-enhanced classrooms. In International conference on artificial intelligence in education (pp. 154-168). Springer, Cham.

Hussain, M., Zhu, W., Zhang, W., & Abidi, S. M. R. (2018). Student engagement predictions in an e-learning system and their impact on student course assessment scores. Computational intelligence and neuroscience, 2018.

Kim, J., Merrill, K., Xu, K., & Sellnow, D. D. (2020). My teacher is a machine: Understanding students' perceptions of AI teaching assistants in online education. International Journal of Human–Computer Interaction, 36(20), 1902-1911.

Kose, H., Kalanee, I., Yildirim, Y., Recovering Higher Education During and After the Pandemic, Chapter 2, Handbook of Researcher on Future of Work and Education: Implications for Curriculum Delivery and Work Design, (2021), 14-26.

Luckin, R., Holmes, W., Griffiths, M., & Forcier, L. B. (2016). Intelligence Unleashed: An Argument for AI in Education.

Lynch, L. (2021, February 04). 4 ways machine learning can improve online education. Retrieved from https://www.learndash.com/4-ways-machine-learning-can-improve-online-education/

Lynch, M. (2018, September 14). Smart seating Charts: The key to better student performance? The Tech Edvocate. https://www.thetechedvocate.org/smart-seating-charts-the-key-to-better-student-performance/.

Murphy, R. F. (2019). Artificial intelligence Applications to Support K-12 Teachers and Teaching. A Review of Promising Applications, Opportunities and Challenges, and Risks. Rand Corporation.

O'Brien, B. (2002). Online student retention: can it be done? (pp. 1479-1483). Association for the Advancement of Computing in Education (AACE).

Ryan, P., Luz, S., Albert, P., Vogel, C., Normand, C., & Elwyn, G. (2019). Using artificial intelligence to assess clinicians' communication skills. Bmj, 364.

Sharma, K., Giannakos, M., & Dillenbourg, P. (2020). Eye-tracking and artificial intelligence to enhance motivation and learning. Smart Learning Environments, 7, 1-19.

Soloviev, V. (2018). Machine learning approach for student engagement automatic recognition from facial expressions. Scientific Publications of the State University of Novi Pazar Series A: Applied Mathematics, Informatics and mechanics, 10(2), 79-86.

Soohoo, S. (2020, November). Artificial intelligence spending quick Look: U.S. buying behavior by industry, company size, and LOB Versus it, 2020. Retrieved from https://www.aws.idc.com/getdoc.jsp?containerId=US47016420

Swan, K. (2002). Building learning communities in online courses: The importance of interaction. Education, Communication & Information, 2(1), 23-49.

Teke, A., Cengiz, E., Çetin, M., Demir, C., Kirkbir, F., & Fedai, T. (2012). Analysis of the multi-item dimensionality of patients' perceived value in hospital services. Journal of medical systems, 36(3), 1301-1307.

Thomas. (2020, August 17). Natural language processing is changing these 5 industries. Retrieved from https://fastdatascience.com/natural-language-processing-is-changing-these-5-industries/

Tortop, H. S. (2015). A comparison of gifted and non-gifted students' self-regulation skills for science learning. Journal for the Education of Gifted Young Scientists, 3(1), 42-57.

True Interaction. (n.d.). *AI and the Classroom: Machine Learning in Education.* True. https:/www.trueinteraction.com/ai-and-the-classroom-machine-learning-in-education/

Wong, C. W., Tsai, A., Jonas, J. B., Ohno-Matsui, K., Chen, J., Ang, M., & Ting, D. S. W. (2021). Digital Screen Time During the Covid-19 Pandemic: Risk for a Further Myopia Boom?. American journal of ophthalmology, 223, 333-337

Practice and Theory Need Each Other for Social Life and Values in Digital Humanities Concept

İbrahim Kurt
Stichting Cosmicus/NL

Abstract

Human beings come to on a common saying for this century's society; it is called "knowledge society". Therefore, the societies are developing on the production of knowledge mainly in this 21st century. It is supported to transfer mainly through education and training with spreading through communication technologies. Education has a big role in every structure of the society.

It is necessary to educate members of the societies who are going to take a roll in "knowledge society". However, people keep in touch more with Digital technologies to get or give more information especially in developed parts of the countries. That is why mainly for their relations and communications have been affected in many parts of the society and its structures between people. People get more information but use less. They have more contacts but see less. They have more connections each other but less relations. They get more knowledge but teach less. They speak more but do less. There can be found "more and less" points from the people, societies, and their relations with each other. Generally, it is shown that in those areas, it makes a big gap between practice and theory. The activities that are planned within the social life to bring training and public education into life in a systematic way. They show themselves as a structure that make individuals earn social rank and teach their roles, supports with the education. It is necessary to make a connection on values, behaviors, and attitudes in social live for human beings. The given education can make them to be gained, so that they can put the things that are learned into practice, embracing the values while covering behaviors.

In this article it has been studied how practice (relations, behaviors, and attitudes) keeps values alive within social life with their own rules.

Key words: Education, Social life, Practice and theory, Values education

London International Conferences

londonic.uk   ukeyconsultingpublishing.co.uk

Humanitarian Dimension of Economic Growth: Problems and Judgments

Taushanzhi Constantine
Comrat State University
taushanzhi47@mail.ru

Abstract

The article focuses on the problems of measuring economic growth. There has been made an attempt to study the qualitative dimension of economic growth. The analysis has revealed that the statistical evaluation reflects only one side in the life of an individual. The laws of economics are incompatible with the laws of nature. Having considered the Solow growth model it has been figured but that it does not correspond to contemporary realities. The essence of the equation is known: $Y=F(K,L)$.

Keywords: Economic growth, new paradigm, non-economic factors, R. Solow, evolution, tradition, religion.